ADVANCE PRAISE FOR THE BOOK

A book to be kept always as a reference for why your projects are not moving in the right direction. I recommend this book not just to Engineers and Managers, but also for Directors to find mismanaged elements coming in the way of their SUCCESS. Well done Manoj, a long-awaited book. All the Best!

—AJAI MISHRA, Retd Project Director, Nuclear Recycle Group Projects, Bhabha Atomic Research Centre, India

Incisive and a well-researched self-help cum business book. Do buy this one to find a solution to all work-related crisis and turn into a master manager at your workplace!

—SUHAIL MATHUR, TEDx Speaker, Author, Literary agent at The Book Bakers.

Author Manoj has explained the key operational risk management techniques in simple yet effective manner to survive in a VUCA world. I recommend this book for Engineers, Project Managers, and Business Leaders!

—SNEHAL FULZELE, CEO and Co-Founder, Cloud Lending Solutions Inc, Master's Degree in Software Engineering, Carnegie Mellon University, USA

A terrific book that bridges the gap between Project management, Quality management, and Technology. Must read by professionals of all industry to delight customers and deliver world-class products or services!

—SANJAY RAM, IIT Mumbai, IIM Kozhikode, ASQ Certified Black Belt, Senior Manager Business Excellence, Vodafone Shared Services

There are so many factors—internal and external, that can derail a project...this book is a SAVIOUR! It also presents powerful strategies that an organisation can adopt to stay ahead of competitors.

—RUTURAJ MOKAL, Welingkar Institute of Management,
ITIL Certified Senior Manager, AtoS Syntel

Managing risk in organisation projects is a tough job...this book exactly gives proposal, scope, quality, technology, and engineering aspects that need to be considered to effectively manage projects.

—SUNIL YADAV, IIT Roorkee, Principal Architect, Dell EMC

This book is a compelling read…almost gives all the risks that could fail my project and how to come out of it.

—ASHISH CHANDORKAR, IIT Delhi, Senior Manager, AtoS Syntel

This is a masterpiece...the book has explained so easily how to run a project successfully and emerge as a leader in the workplace!

—SUDHAKAR MISHRA, Manager, Infosys

Manoj uses his rich diverse experience and demonstrates his research in unconquered landscapes of business and management world. The book covers in-depth strategies for project success and delighting customers. Must read for fast forward progress in career!

—DIPEN JOSHI, ITIL and CSM Certified Senior Manager, AtoS Syntel

An engaging journey that uncovers all practical aspects of why a project or organisation fails to attain objectives in the real world—must buy for success in information technology and related industry!

—DEBANJAN CHAKRABORTY, AINS Certified Insurance Expert,
Senior Business Analyst, Cognizant

Extremely pleased to have found a book that explains all the software engineering, quality, and management aspects of the company projects in detail!

—UPENDRA SAHU, Solution Architect, Birlasoft

This book has in-depth coverage of what fails a project; at the same time, it helps to mitigate and prevent such risks...highly useful and a must buy!

—RIDDHI KUBAL, Manager, Majesco Inc

Covers almost all the factors than can impact an organisation. Extremely useful for managers like us...in delivering things with quality to clients.

—AMOL SHINDE, Manager, Alliance Insurance Brokers

This book is a one of its kind...it covers nearly all quality aspects that projects need as part of compliance in the IT and related industry.

—LALIT GHANIRA, ISO Certified Lead Auditor,
Team Lead Quality, VitalHealth Software

The book looks at things from the organisation and top managements viewpoint and is thus useful for any enterprise. Excellent read for all private or government sector employees, managers, and the leaders!

—SHAILESH KUMAR, Government Employee,
Bhabha Atomic Research Centre

This book covers all major risks that we as quality assurance team members experience in day-to-day life while running our projects. The testing risks associated are also covered in detail.

—GAURAV OCHANI, Member of Technical Staff, TIBCO Software

A paradise of knowledge for new generation hi-tech students for understanding business, management, and technology insights. Must have on your bookshelf for quick professional success!

—RAMA SHETTY, Senior Teacher, Atomic Energy Education Society, Mumbai

I found this book very interesting to read...now I can understand the theory behind the software engineering subjects better...also it gave me a fair idea of how to do things right in information technology industry.

—RITU, B Tech Computer Science, Indraprastha College for Women, University of Delhi

101 SECRETS OF PROJECT RISK MANAGEMENT

101 SECRETS OF PROJECT RISK MANAGEMENT

MANOJ YADAV

Vitasta

Published by
Renu Kaul Verma
Vitasta Publishing Pvt Ltd
2/15, Ansari Road, Daryaganj
New Delhi-110 002
info@vitastapublishing.com

ISBN 978-93-86473-65-3

First Edition 2019
Second Reprint 2021
MRP ₹595

Editor: Veena Batra
Cover and layout by Somesh Kumar Mishra
Printed by Chaman Enterprises

You have to enable and empower people to make decisions independent of you. As I've learned, each person on a team is an extension of your leadership; if they feel empowered by you, they will magnify your power to lead.

—Tom Ridge,
Politician and Author,
Former Governor of Pennsylvania, USA

SEVEN THINGS THIS BOOK WILL HELP YOU ACHIEVE

- Delivering world-class products/services.
- Winning your customers/clients.
- Surviving the disruptions.
- Maximising your organisation's profits.
- Strengthening your company market reputation.
- Making you efficient and effective at work.
- Leading you on a definite path to success in your profession.

CONTENTS

ACKNOWLEDGEMENTS

This work of knowledge and art has been possible with the divine blessings of lord Ganesha, who was always in my mind while I was writing the book. Jesus—you gave me strength and courage to withstand the adversities of life.

Dedicated to my son Akshaj, and my family for standing by me in my tough and good times, and always believing in me.

A very special thanks to the 16+ beautiful souls and well-wishers (names mentioned in the 'Advance praise for the book' section), who gave their precious time from their busy schedule to go through the manuscript of this book and offered valuable suggestions apart from praising the book.

I would like to express my sincere gratitude to eminent literary agent, Suhail Mathur, who was the first person from the publishing world to believe in my work and selected it for representation to esteemed publishers through his glorious agency, *The Book Bakers*.

Words would not be enough to thank the founder and Managing Director, Ms Renu Kaul Verma of Vitasta Publishing Pvt Ltd, India, and author and editor Bill K Koul who found this book extremely useful. They have made my dream of making a difference in the life of millions come true, by presenting this opportunity to me.

Thanks to my editor Syeda FR who helped me make this manuscript better and Veena Batra, my editor at Vitasta for fine-tuning it further and being extremely supportive during the entire process of publishing.

FOREWORD

What's the probability of you bumping into a random guy in a bookstore, who is writing a book on executing projects smoothly? Tough call, isn't it?

But it happened! The bookstore chat quickly became professional association & I had the privilege to see this book beforehand.

Manoj Yadav presents a book YOU always wanted, with his decades of intense, diverse experience in a VUCA world.

101 Secrets Of Project Risk Management is highly relevant, detailed, simple, skilfully presented, & jargon free book.

From discovering risks ahead of times to altogether eliminating them, it becomes your user's manual. I recommend this to be in your office handbag, all the time.

If we would have had such a book in our times, our work-life balance would have been a different story!

A stitch in time saves nine, but Manoj Yadav offers you one hundred more!

Happy Project execution!

Rajesh S Angal, PfMP, PMP, Trained 1700+ professionals
Head – Corp Project Portfolio & Talent Management
Tata Consulting Engineers Limited

INTRODUCTION

Why use 101 secrets of project risk management?

Few Project Management Facts of the Real World

- *According to an IBM study, only 40% of projects meet schedule, budget and quality goals. Further, they found that the biggest barriers to success are people factors.*
- *The Portland Business Journal found similarly depressing statistics: 'Most analyses conclude that between 65 and 80% of IT projects fail to meet their objectives, and also run significantly late or cost far more than planned.'*
- *Geneca, a software development company, noted from its studies that 'fuzzy business objectives, out-of-sync stakeholders and excessive rework mean that 75% of project participants lack confidence that their projects will succeed.'*
- *KPMG New Zealand found that 'an incredible 70% of organisations have suffered at least one project failure in the prior 12 months and 50% of respondents indicated that their project failed to consistently achieve what they had set out to achieve.'*

Project management as seen from the above statistics and research is a tough job. Therefore, professionals who have years of experience still face problems or challenges when working on projects. Also, *when it comes to managing operational risks in a project, they are unsure mainly because there are rarely books out there in the market that can help to survive the VUCA world at work place which is driven by volatility, uncertainty, complexity, and ambiguity.*

So, the big question is—Is there an art of managing projects successfully?

Yes, definitely. Currently project management, quality management, and technology (which actually enables one to solve the business needs) are different topics to study for professionals, though all are interrelated. These are vast topics which makes it difficult for the managers and project team who are from engineering or management background to plan and execute projects well.

How about having a book that can address the issues related to all of the above areas in one book? A book that can come in handy when managing all aspects of an organisation project and survive the VUCA scenario which is a common thing at workplace.

The premises of VUCA tend to shape an organisation's capacity to:-

- ✓ Anticipate the issues that take shape with time
- ✓ Understand the consequences of issues and actions
- ✓ Appreciate the interdependence of variables
- ✓ Prepare for alternative realities and challenges
- ✓ Interpret and address relevant opportunities

101 Secrets Of Project Risk Management is a unique book that is written to solve all above challenges of a project in one book. The book is structured in such a way that it will help to make better project decisions. It thus teaches you to do effective planning and execution of projects at workplace.

It is a comprehensive book that presents you a practical approach towards project management rather than focusing on theoretical aspects. The strategies given can be implemented from day one to save from 98% factors that impact your projects and ensure smooth operations.

How the book solves this?

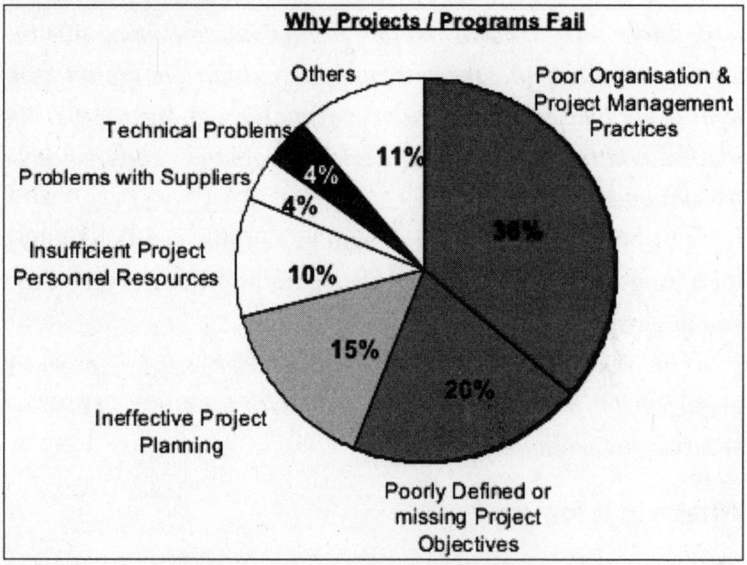

Source: Standish Group International, Survey from 2500 personnel attending project management training.

It can be figured out from the above chart, that in every problem whether due to poor planning, missing objectives, supplier issues, poor management practices, and others leading to project failure the primary cause is the *'people factor'* in an organisation.

The risks, therefore, that can occur in project management have been arranged in 9 chapters by classifying the 101 classes of risks or challenges into 'sources' of risk. These sources are nothing but the various interfaces or components of a project from which a risk that can derail a project arise. These could be infrastructure setup, project scope, its leadership, technology and tools, customer/client, processes, external environment changes, project team, and not striving for competitive edge.

With each risk, highlighted are the 'prevention strategies' or steps you can take to mitigate the impact of risk to the project.

Proactively implementing the prevention strategies given in the book under each risk will improve project outcome, maximise the organisation's revenue, increase customer satisfaction, protect from legal issues that can arise, enhance reputation of organisation in market, and help in delivering world class products and services to the customers.

The book is designed to remain in a professional's handbag for a long time. It is a map to keep coming back to every time you are lost on your road to success.

The book is written with vendor or service provider management in mind, when they work with customers in product or service-based industry.

What's in it for you?

If managing or working on a project appears a tough job, this book is for you as it's going to make it very simple. If you are a professional or entrepreneur in your early 30s or 40s and are confused by how great companies deliver world-class products or services, what quality culture can be acquired to stay ahead in future or to stay ahead of the competitors, then this book will answer all such questions.

If you are baffled by how greater customer satisfaction can be achieved or what are the secrets to satisfy client or customer, then this book is for you. If you are going to appear for any well recognised global certifications in project management, operational management, quality management, or MBA project management exams, consider reading this book first so that you gain deeper understanding of practical issues and challenges affecting organisation projects. This will enable you to understand the theoretical and practical aspects of those exams better. In case you have completed such certifications with flying colours, still this book is for you as it gives a revolutionary approach to manage projects.

The intended audience includes professionals—from business leaders at the top to mid-level executives including the *just starters*. The book is also equally useful for any entrepreneur as managing business is like managing small to large projects.

At the same time, the book is for students of MBA in Project Management, MBA in Information Technology, Engineering branches like Computer Science, Information Technology, Software Engineering, Systems Engineering, and Project Engineering. Also, those interested in Operations management, Quality management, Operational risk management, IT risk management, Enterprise risk management (ERM), or has zeal to learn will find this book very useful.

Lastly, in the words of my favourite philanthropist, Bill Gates, founder—Bill and Melinda Gates foundation and Microsoft:-

It's fine to celebrate success but it is more important to heed the lessons of failure.

This book is a compilation of all such lessons. Welcome to this beautiful journey of what all can derail your project and how to overcome such challenges.

Wishing you success! Hoping to hear from you how this book helped you in achieving success in your career. Do write to me at *authormanoj.y@gmail.com*

Manoj Yadav
Mumbai, March 2019

WHEN YOU DON'T INVEST IN INFRASTRUCTURE, YOU ARE GOING TO PAY SOONER OR LATER.

—MIKE PARKER

CHAPTER 01 INFRASTRUCTURE SETUP

INFRASTRUCTURE includes facilities, hardware, software, networks, data center, and human resources which are basic elements required to run business operations and support the services provided by an organisation to its clients.

Vertical or Business units (BUs) are set up by the organisation to carry out different kinds of services for multiple clients. These verticals are divided into *projects,* which are nothing but temporary endeavours to create a unique product, service, or result as requested by the clients.

This chapter explores risks due to delay in infrastructure setup, licensing, resourcing or staffing challenges, colocation, and security issues that are faced while working in projects. It also outlines strategies to prevent or mitigate them.

Risk #1–Delay in infrastructure, environment setup, and access on award of contract

Infrastructure is much more important than architecture.

–Rem Koolhaas

Let's say you as a 'project manager' receive and win the bid for a new project from a client. Before the project even starts, you need infrastructure like dedicated secured development facility with seating arrangements for resources, conference rooms, computers, conference phones, network, etc. All these activities related to infrastructure require time and should be well set up as per the client's demands prior to even starting work upon your project, else it will delay things and impact the schedule, the project cost and trust factor with the client leading to non-compliance issues with the contract terms and can become a reason for the cancellation of the project itself.

Prevention strategy

- Get in touch with your other departments like admin, HR and technical support team to ensure infrastructure readiness in advance before actual work starts on the project.
- Create priority list of all the activities that need to be implemented as part of the initiation phase and plan the timelines for set-up activities.
- Take necessary approvals from concerned directors of individual departments.
- Always keep all the stakeholders informed of initial set-up activities and associated slippage from the planned schedule due to any delay in set-up and security access measures.
- Plan to work extra hours or on weekends if there is considerable delay to meet the schedule or extend impacted milestones of the project; inform the client with due justification for the same.

Risk #2–Delay in set up at offshore due to software licensing issues

> ***In the epic war over Silicon Valley's intellectual property, Bill Gates was on the side of licensing copyright and robust protections for intellectual property. He wasn't on the side of the hackers, and he didn't want information to be free.***
>
> **–Franklin Foer**

Commercial softwares mostly have a license for using them over a certain period and your company has to pay the owner of these software products for using the services. Not using genuine software or using pirated versions can entangle your company in legal battle involving costly intellectual property rights (IP) or copyright laws. This can be very expensive for your company. So, you need to ensure that you use genuine software products with valid license.

Generally, once software license expires, you cannot use the software any more, but there are many proprietary softwares in the market that can charge a higher rate on usage after the license expires. So, you need to be very careful. Also, organisations which are large may need to have a technical department with officers who can look after licensing issues, so that work is not affected and any kind of ignorance does not eat up your profits.

Prevention strategy

- Planning for the software and hardware licenses is to be done at the early stage prior to when project actually starts. Sufficient time and budget for purchasing the licensed software products needs to be allocated for the same.
- Organisations to invest in database software tools like Software Asset Management by Microsoft, or Flex-Net Manager by Flexera Software where license attributes can be recorded in the database and monitored. Automatic trigger thus generated by the database tool for particular software indicates that the renewal process can be started for it.
- Software license auditor tool can be purchased by your company. These auditor tools can run over the company network and identify the deployed license issues across all systems in a network.
- Management needs to be informed of any impact on the schedule and cost due to licensing issues when a project

team is unable to work. Also, to minimise the impact, check if project resources can continue the work from some other machines or locations for a temporary period.

- Nowadays, there are many software products which are available at minimal cost in the market—open-source software (OSS) and free software. Check if these can be utilised so that work is not affected and expenses are reduced.
- Do inform the client when major impact happens and check with them for alternative solutions.

Risk #3–Human resource or staffing challenges in projects

Research indicates that workers have three prime needs: Interesting work, recognition for doing a good job and being let in on things that are going on in the company.

–Zig Ziglar

Human resources are the most important asset of any organisation or project. The right selection of candidates will help you to reach project goal on time and complete it within the budget.

Staffing primarily gets affected when your company does not have a good image in the society. People do not want to be a part of a company or industry that has a bad reputation in the market in terms of nature of work that's been carried out, remuneration that's paid to the employees, job security, work environment, working hours, recognition of employees, prejudices while hiring or when working in a company, quality of delivery your company provides to customers, reputation with customers, and limited growth plans of a company. The interest of candidates for joining such companies keeps on declining with time and project managers are not able to find the right candidate to fill their project positions.

Some of the major staffing challenges faced by an organisation are inability to fill all project positions, referred to as *understaffing*, not able to attract skilled resources in the market, keeping staff motivated, keeping them trained in relevant organisational skills, and retaining talent.

Prevention strategy

- Managers to get in touch with their HR department for resource hiring from the market or from other internal projects in a company itself. Ensure proper Job Description (JD) is drafted by the project manager and given to HR for finding suitable candidates, arranging interviews and processing the CV of the candidates.
- Avoid more than two rounds of interviews. The first stage to be a telephonic interview to filter out the unworthy candidates; to reduce inconvenience to both the parties in terms of effort, money, and time. Finally, a face-to-face interview where final candidate can be selected by the manager. Having more than two rounds can be frustrating for the candidates. At the same time, it questions the credibility of the organisation's other two rounds and the selection committee involved in them.
- HR to draft fair staffing policies, employees' code of conduct, and good practices for the organisation. Management needs to ensure these are implemented at the project level too.
- Management needs to ensure that the resources are occupied in the project through proper delegation and task tracking. They can be allocated to a new project immediately once an assignment ends.
- Promote training of the employees in existing and new technology so that resources remain relevant throughout the duration of the project as technology and tools may undergo changes at a rapid rate.
- Attrition issues to be addressed by making effort to retain

the personnel by motivating them and fulfilling the benefits that employees seek which could include giving onsite opportunities, better emoluments or a better role. Win-win situation for both the employer and the employee to be considered. Moreover, the high attrition issues need to be analysed to understand the exact problem areas and proper corrective actions to be taken for the same.

- Managers to maintain and track the resources getting-in or going-out of the project for the entire duration of the project. Take appropriate action to fill the positions demanded in the contract and take corrective action when any staffing issues are observed. Share good practices and ideas between the teams. Leaders to share success stories to motivate employees to achieve their best.
- Survey your employees for engagement regularly. This helps as a feedback mechanism to improve things further and create a good corporate environment.

Risk #4–Inability to colocate resources

Growth is never by mere chance; it is the result of forces working together.

–James Cash Penney

Colocation, often referred to as a 'tight matrix', means all the resources or team members of a project are located in the same single location.

It enables face-to-face communication with team members leading to better interaction, effective coordination in work, sharing ideas and expertise, which ultimately leads to producing exceptional quality products. So, this is often used as a strategic way to maximise productivity in an organisation.

However, a project can increase in size when you win more business from the client. This can call for bigger team size and large space to continue your project operations. It can be difficult for your organisation to make arrangements for common location for all the resources due to costing and space constraints as in metro cities like Mumbai and New York. At times, existing project location can have constraints like space, network or security issues. Moreover, the resources can have their personal commitments.

All the factors discussed above demand from a manager to spread the team across multiple locations. However, this can hamper effective participation between the resources, affecting their productivity, output, and quality that can be achieved when working together.

Colocation and multilocation needs are often specified as part of your contract with the customers.

Prevention strategy

- Gauge the amount of coordination required within your team members of the project by understanding the type of work and complexity of the project. Do talk with the client and understand any *colocation* needs as per the contract.
- If *colocation* is specified as part of a contract, management to look for better facility with larger space where all the team members can sit near each other, collaborate effectively, and work as a team.
- If *multilocation* is not an issue with the client, team members can be shifted to alternate locations as desired by the management.
- Forecasting of the resources can be used as tool to come up with the additional space required in the future in advance. Also, costing and risk associated with new facility to be considered before planning to shift to new facility.
- In the modern world, however, a multilocation team

is no more a constraint. For effective participation and communication within the team members even in multilocation scenario, many solutions are available in the market. Adequate internal telephone, mailing facility with adequate mailbox size, software tools that allow sharing for the desktop, video conferencing, and chatting applications can be purchased. These greatly facilitate interaction and communication between the project team members.

- Also, having a multilocation team reduces many of the risks to your project due to:-
  - ✓ *Natural disasters like flooding, heavy rains, political riots or agitations* which may halt your colocated project for multiple days or stop the work in totality, thereby leading to delay in shipping the product to the client.
  - ✓ *Not finding the right candidate with necessary skills and experience* as in one particular location like Mumbai, or New York, you may not have adequate number of candidates with requisite skills and experience, a risk that colocated project managers often face.

So, choose colocation or multilocation teams carefully by evaluating on different parameters as discussed above, the risks involved, and the expectation from the client.

Risk #5–Not having a secure environment and best security practices

There are only two types of companies: those that have been hacked, and those that will be.

–Robert Mueller

A project needs to be conducted in an environment that has good security in terms of protecting the physical assets and electronic assets. *Confidentiality, Integrity, and Availability (CIA)* are the heart of information security. You need to ensure these parameters are always intact in your project at all times for establishing strict security guidelines.

- ✓ *Confidentiality*—confidentiality ensures that information is not disclosed to unauthorised individuals, entities, or processes.
- ✓ *Integrity*—assuring the accuracy, completeness, and consistency of data.
- ✓ *Availability*—data from the information system to be readily available when needed.

For information security, the project should be conducted in secure environments, following security guidelines, and dos and don'ts given in the contract by the client. In addition, it should have *data security guidelines* and arrangements in place for backup and restoration.

Based on whether your client is in banking, payment, insurance, healthcare, manufacturing or any other sector, you need to put right security standards, relevant to industry-type, data compliance, and practices.

Example:

a) Payment industry needs to be compliant with the Payment Card Industry Data Security Standard (PCI DSS).

b) Healthcare with (Health Insurance Portability and Accountability Act) HIPPA.

These standards can also vary from country to country in terms of whether your healthcare company is located in USA or Europe.

In addition, sharing client or customer data internally in your company or with another party can lead to security breach or data compliance issues. Clients prefer working with service providers that are ISO 27001 certified in information security management.

Prevention strategy

- Have any specific infrastructure needs for security drafted in the *master service agreement (MSA)* itself with your client while drafting the contract. Guidelines for general access security, data, physical or electronic security needs to be drafted in organisation's policy. Also, access roles and escalation mechanism for handling security incident to be planned.
- For environment security, ensure well-spaced infrastructure facility with security guards, registry entry maintained, smart-card, equipped with fire alarms, etc.
- A good company should have well-drafted information security policy, internal dos and don'ts in place, clean desk policy, password and recovery guidelines for handling client data in place. Client related project data is not to be shared or discussed with other project teams. Proper verification through ready questionnaire to be followed by project team members or on-call support team before sharing data with outsiders.
- Have strict sanctions for violating these policy guidelines that include warnings, monetary penalties, and even termination based on the severity of the violations.
- Use desktops having firewalls, antivirus software, and other important security software installed to prevent worms, viruses, and trojans from entering your system via the web or external media. Only genuine licensed software products and tools to be purchased.
- *The first line of defense is of course the employees.* Project teams can take the following measures in the premises to prevent security issues.
    - ✓ Log off machine when not in use and do not share your credentials—user id and password with other employees in same facility.
    - ✓ Best practices in a project for classifying documents or data at all times to be used like following standards of classifying

each artifact into *confidential, public, or private.*

- ✓ Always ensuring that old project data which is not used by anyone is archived or destroyed.
- ✓ Never visit the websites which are unknown or irrelevant to your profession. Ensure HTTPS based websites for browsing are used rather than just HTTP as these use SSL certificate for authentication, which are relatively safe.
- ✓ Never open email file attachments from unknown entities. Also, team should not make company email ids public, over the social media sites like Facebook, Twitter, or Google nor use these for sharing information with outsiders

- Training by internal security teams on periodic basis to be conducted for the company employees and the project team members.
- Security audits to be conducted periodically adhering to international standards like ISO 27001 and gaps found by the auditor to be closed by project manager on priority basis.

Risk #6–Infrastructure changes in the middle of the project due to vendor management or client demands

Technology is characterised by constant change, rapid innovation, creative destruction, and revolutionary products.

–Marsha Blackburn

Your company VP may demand replacement of all your company's computer machines with the latest machines of Lenovo or HP and may also seek some different versions of operating system like Windows 10. In addition, they may plan to revamp the networks, antivirus replacements, seating arrangements, etc.

Not just internal executives but your client also may demand upgradation activities while the project is running at full speed. All these decisions could hamper ongoing project activities impacting the schedule and cost.

Prevention strategy

- Get in touch with your technical support team. Request them to carry out replacement activities at night, especially on weekends and long weekends so as to ensure minimal impact on regular project deliveries.
- Consider opting for phased releases rather than doing it all at a single time. One-time replacement can delay regular project delivery for many days; also, any compatibility issue in the new software and hardware installed may bring the project to a standstill for days impacting budget and schedule. Various strategies for phased releases can be used like carrying it project wise, location wise, or the way machines and servers are networked or configured.
- Measure the impact on schedule and cost. Escalate to senior management indicating impact on project deliverables.
- Consider switching to a new location for temporary period or another facility in your existing premises. Utilise buffer resources available in the project for minimal impact on deliveries. Motivate the team to stretch for few days if required.
- Keep all the stakeholders informed of associated delays in setup and access. Inform the client of any change in cost or schedule and ask support from them when need arises.

Risk #7–System outages due to virus attacks, technical faults, or network issues

The secret of crisis management is not good vs bad, it's preventing the bad from getting worse.

–Andy Gilman

Network outages and downtime issues can be caused due to:-

✓ Faults, errors or exceptions in network devices

- ✓ Configuration changes in network device like router, gateways
- ✓ Operational human errors
- ✓ Mismanagement of devices
- ✓ Network congestion
- ✓ Power outages
- ✓ Server hardware failure
- ✓ Security attacks such as denial of service (DoS)
- ✓ Failed software and firmware upgrade or patches
- ✓ Incompatibility between firmware and hardware device
- ✓ Unnatural disasters and mishaps on the network such as a minor accident, cable cut due to rodent attack, etc.

Such issues when not controlled can lead to important data loss for clients, information security issues, or loss of productivity that can eventually force them to switch to other vendors or cause legal trouble for you.

Prevention strategy

- System and network services to be considered from reliable service provider only. Inventory of all physical and electronic resources—software tools, databases, human resources used in the project to be maintained and monitored for system performance.
- High security environment for protecting physical and electronic assets to be in place. Request your technical support team for the same.
- Have *business continuity plan (BCP) or disaster recovery plan (DRP)* in place and a recovery team for carrying out the strategies documented in them, so as to continue the deliveries even if a temporary disaster occurs. This recovery team to be tested from time to time for carrying out strategies documented to avoid losses when such outages actually happen. Adequate back-up servers, software systems, and

hardware to be in place to recover and restore the application systems to their initial state prior to outages.

- Also, there are many companies out there in the market providing infrastructure support through cloud service medium and now even database maintenance service can also be outsourced. Consider utilising these specialised services as initial investment, maintenance cost, and disruption in service to your facilities due to such outsourcing will be close to none and is far better than owning servers, networks, database management system (DBMS) and then maintaining them.
- During outage, manager to escalate to the technical support teams for resolving the issues at the earliest. When outage is for significant duration and is affecting deliverables, manager to inform the client for the same and re-plan the schedule.
- Alternate location team at offshore or at onsite can take over responsibility of the important deliverables. For the loss of time, team can be asked to stretch for extra hours.
- *Configuration management* audits on periodic basis to be arranged to verify any lapses in processes and preventing future issues.
- *Dispose of any electronic waste in a timely manner.*

Risk #8–Application link performance issues

We are all now connected by the Internet, like neurons in a giant brain.
–Stephen Hawking

Application links like Citrix are used to connect to the client environment and gain access to their machines, servers, files, database, and storage system for carrying out development and testing activities.

With the introduction of *cloud-based service model,* many of the infrastructure services are now online and are in cloud mode. Many companies are using cloud-based services today as cost-effective way of running their business, storing data, and accessing the execution environment, which is why link connection applications have gained even more importance than in the past.

Links and networks are therefore required to be up and running at all times, as this can severely impact the business of your client and company.

Prevention strategy

- Technical glitches to be reported to the technical hardware and software support department of the company who can look into the issues or monitor the load on all the links to identify potential reasons of performance issues. Project teams to work with business recovery and tech support teams in making some alternate arrangements.
- Check if resources can be utilised to finish deliverables in the limited time once system is up and running after some time. Ask your team to stretch few more hours to accommodate for the lost time, if required.
- If significant impact on the project due to outage, inform the client for appropriate measures from their side. They can come up with an action plan for you to deal with the same. Reschedule the milestones and update the delivery plans.

Risk #9–Unavailability of shared folder in a project due to security or compliance issues

Use an Online File Sharing tool to stop losing track of the project documents, keep track of the latest versions, and access them from anywhere.

–Tony Zink

Shareable secure folder is needed to keep the artifacts or deliverables which are produced during the life cycle of a project. This is used by the team for keeping knowledge documents on application or product, domain knowledge, technical skills, lessons learnt, and delivery related artifacts. All these help the team members to update their knowledge, remain relevant, and in driving continual improvements in projects.

Not having one will lead to knowledge management, configuration management, and delivery issues in the project.

Prevention strategy

- Vendor project team to request the client for shared path folder or online file sharing tool required for artifacts management with secure access. If access to client shared path folder is allowed by the client, project team to keep artifacts there in client environment.
- Client or vendor to enable controlled access to repository, its folders, and documents. Alterations of the artifacts to be allowed to certain project roles only.
- In case the client company does not provide shared folder due to some security reason, your vendor company itself can provide one. However, the same needs to have permission from the client as they often consider it as risk to data security or compliance.
- Backup of the folder to be maintained on a periodic basis so as to restore the original after a data loss event.

A GOOD PROBLEM
STATEMENT OFTEN INCLUDES
WHAT IS KNOWN,
WHAT IS UNKNOWN AND
WHAT IS SOUGHT.
—EDWARD HODNETT

CHAPTER

02 SCOPE BASED CHALLENGES

SCOPE is what defines a product or service in a project. It is given in the agreement of contract called *Statement of Work (SOW)* between the client and the service provider company. High level business requirements given in SOW form the basis of scope.

Master Service Agreement (MSA) is a legal contract that governs relationship between the service provider and the client. All significant expectations between the parties like payment terms, confidentiality, delivery requirements, warranties, work standards, ownership of IP rights, dispute resolution, etc. are drafted in the contract and agreed by both the parties. It also serves as basis for awarding multiple SOWs with different scope.

This chapter covers the risks like SOW contract not drafted properly, requirement lacking depth, business requirements not matching the business case, poor architectural design, scope creep, and gold plating issues along with strategies to deal with them.

Risk #10–SOW contract not drafted properly and lacks details

You sign an agreement; you make a contract; you live up to it. You never get what you deserve. You get what you negotiate. You got a right to say yay or nay.

–Don King

SOW contract between the client and the service provider is enforceable in the legal system. It forms a basis of the benefits one party is promising to another party.

A typical SOW comprises of following sections:-

- ✓ *Purpose of the project or its scope.* It covers what product or application system the vendor project team needs to develop, maintain, or support. The different project activities, and reporting they need to perform. The *in-scope* and *out-of-scope* activities are also stated clearly in the contract.
- ✓ *Type of contract* like fixed price (FP), time and material (T&M), cost plus fee (CPF), and cost-plus award fee (CPAF).
- ✓ *Acceptance criteria* about the deliverables and who will give sign-off/assurance of the intermediate deliverables.
- ✓ *Milestones schedule, deliverables, escalation mechanism, project roles along with their numbers, and the client budget involved.*

It should be signed by both the parties for validity of contract in the legal system and to avoid any disputes between the parties while the project is in execution or thereafter. Not delivering work as promised in the scope or delivering poor quality product may attract legal lawsuits and penalty.

If SOW is not drafted properly, it would create confusion of what exactly the stakeholders need to achieve—as the end result and the objectives of project will be unclear.

Prevention strategy

- Draft your contract well by discussing with the client and other stakeholders. Ensure details about scope, timeline, budget, etc. as discussed above are clearly mentioned and tie payments to milestones.
- Be clear about quality and post production needs.
- Ensure assumptions if any are explicitly mentioned in the contract.

- Use language that everyone can understand. Keep it simple, precise, and clean.
- Get this contract reviewed by the senior management, the client partners, and the legal team of your company. Accommodate their suggestions and negotiate well with the client team.

Risk #11–Business requirements don't match the business case

We welcome this project for its scope and potential.

–Koichiro Matsuura

'*Business requirements*' are nothing but the documentation of customer needs and expectations which are part of the scope document. On the other hand, '*business case*' is a formal document with justification of the proposed project on the basis of expected commercial benefit.

While some may think that '*business case*' is written first, others may argue '*business requirements*' are written first.

Example:

Case1: ***If business case is developed first and high-level business requirements later, then without knowing all high-level requirements the business justification developed for it might be incomplete as problem, opportunity, or product needs are not fully understood.***

Case 2: ***Writing business requirement first and then business case may lack requirements that address what the business needs as benefits, the purpose for which the product needs to be created, the saving it's going to provide, the performance it intends to achieve or the convenience it's going to provide to the customers.***

Both the cases discussed above can impact the project as the project scope or outcomes are not fully understood leading to high rework which may blow up project costing and schedule somewhere in the later stages.

Prevention strategy

- Always as the best practice, develop business case and high-level business requirements together hand-in-hand. This will ensure that business needs are well understood and your project is initiated based on actual customer needs desired in a product.
- Involve the *domain experts* at the early stage so as to draft the high-level business requirements by interviewing the business users, sponsor, and other stakeholders. This will ensure sufficient completeness, and clarity in the business case which will help to gain confidence from the sponsor and the business users.
- Do ensure *traceability of all business cases to business requirements* and vice versa, so as to ensure each of those artifacts complement each other and are in agreement. Any significant change in one of them will impact the other till product is not completed.
- Get these reviewed by the sponsor and other stakeholders.

Risk #12–Requirements lack depth and relevance or are inadequate

Understanding the needs of a business is the starting point for any project.

–John Williams

Sub-standard or poor-quality product will be developed if requirements are not drafted adequately as part of the scope. Also, as requirement related issues are very costly in the later phases ensure they all are minimised and taken due care of in the requirement phase itself.

Some of the major requirement issues observed are:-

- ✓ *Non-compliant requirements*—requirements are not in compliance with laws, regulations, industry standards, and best practices.
- ✓ *Silo requirements*—requirements fail to consider all aspects of project or product, its integration with other application systems, business processes, and database.
- ✓ *Superficial or naive requirements*—lack of due diligence in developing and validating requirements. For example—*subject matter experts (SME)* aren't consulted.
- ✓ *Incorrect requirement priorities*—nice-to-have requirements are classified as high priority.

Prevention strategy

- Always ensure that requirements are provided by those who are experts in business domains and technology. Get help of the domain experts, technical experts, experienced users, and regulatory consultants while framing the requirements. Drafting requirements with person or groups with no specialty or having partial knowledge can lead to incomplete requirements and ultimately a poor product that lacks essential functionalities.
- Interview the business users and intended customers. Brainstorm with them to understand the complete requirements. Utilise other techniques like prototyping, quality function deployment (QFD) and facilitated application specification technique (FAST) for better results.
- Ensure the requirements are in compliance with laws, regulations, industry standards, and best practices.
- Ensure localisation aspects are duly taken care of wherever necessary.
- Learn from competitors' already existing systems—this will help you to understand and frame your requirements well.
- Use prioritisation technique to classify the requirements that

are of more value to the business. Some of the techniques are discussed below. This is important and comes in handy when understanding requirements and to deliver solutions as per the spending budget client can afford.

Prioritisation techniques

MoSCoW Analysis:

This categorises functionalities into Must-have, Should-have, Could-have, and Won't-have features. 'Should' or 'Could' features can be dropped later when delivery timescales or budget are threatened.

- ✓ *Must-have—critical features in a product.*
- ✓ *Should-have—important but not necessary for delivery in current delivery time box.*
- ✓ *Could-have—desirable but not necessary.*
- ✓ *Won't-have—agreed by stakeholders as least critical items with lowest payback and not appropriate to have this time.*

Kano Analysis:

Similar to the above technique but divides requirements into delighters, satisfiers, dissatisfiers, and indifferent.

100-Point Method:

Uses voting for features from customers to arrive at what's best, second best, and so on.

- Develop a prototype of your products early, develop presentations with screen and functionalities of your product and give demo to business users, client, and other stakeholders to validate business requirements. Accommodate any suggestions or feedback for further improvements.
- Get your requirements approved by stakeholders, any suggestion by them to be considered for further improvements.

Risk #13–Not able to manage the requirements

Before product/market fit, your only job that matters is to build a great product.

–Sam Altman

Requirements, whether functional or non-functional, are important and are not to be missed, as they define your product characteristics or behaviour. Any kind of miscommunication or mismanagement by stakeholders can lead to issues in a project in later phases.

Managing requirements is important as it greatly:-

- ✓ Reduces the cost, as defect cost drastically increases with time.
- ✓ Improves quality.
- ✓ Ensures delivery as per project timelines.

Prevention strategy

- Walkthrough of requirement—*high* or *low-level* to be done involving the client and all other stakeholders like *subject matter experts (SME)* or *business analysts (BA)* early in the initiation phase of the project.
- All requirements to be clearly drafted in the requirement document after brainstorming with different stakeholders. Any assumption made to be documented.
- Once all the stakeholders are in agreement, it needs to be reviewed and approved by appropriate authority. Any ambiguity if found, should be resolved during walkthrough and status calls.
- Use *clarification logs* for tracking queries—questions asked, suggested solutions, date of query raised, date of resolution provided are some of the attributes needed to be tracked for better clarity and efficiency of purpose.

- Establish robust *change management process* to manage any new changes in requirements.
- Traceability and version control tools to be utilised for mapping detailed low-level requirement with the high-level business requirements and controlling changes.
- Analyse defects due to requirements in different phases and put corrective actions to improve further.

Risk #14–Poor system architectural design

> ***I strive for two things in design: simplicity and clarity. Great design is born of these two things.***
>
> ***–Lindon Leader***

The high-level business requirements given by the client as part of a scope are translated into technical design by engineers, architects, and scientists. This is often referred to as *design document* and gives the architecture of the software system.

Design document elaborates on impacted screen layouts, their behaviours, interaction with other systems, and flow of programs. The *use case diagram* will help making things visible to customers and provide clarity about the conceived product. In fact, *'design is nothing but thinking made visual'*, rightly said Saul Bass, American graphic designer, and Academy Award winning filmmaker.

Inability to breakdown requirements into detailed design, not able to consider aspects of technology well, missed scenarios or missed use cases, and incorrect algorithms can lead to incomplete product or bugs in the delivered product in later stages which can become a costly affair.

Prevention strategy

- Understand your requirements well, ask questions, do

a thorough impact analysis of the existing product or application system to define the problem and collect as much information about the system. A typical design process comprises of six steps as shown below:-

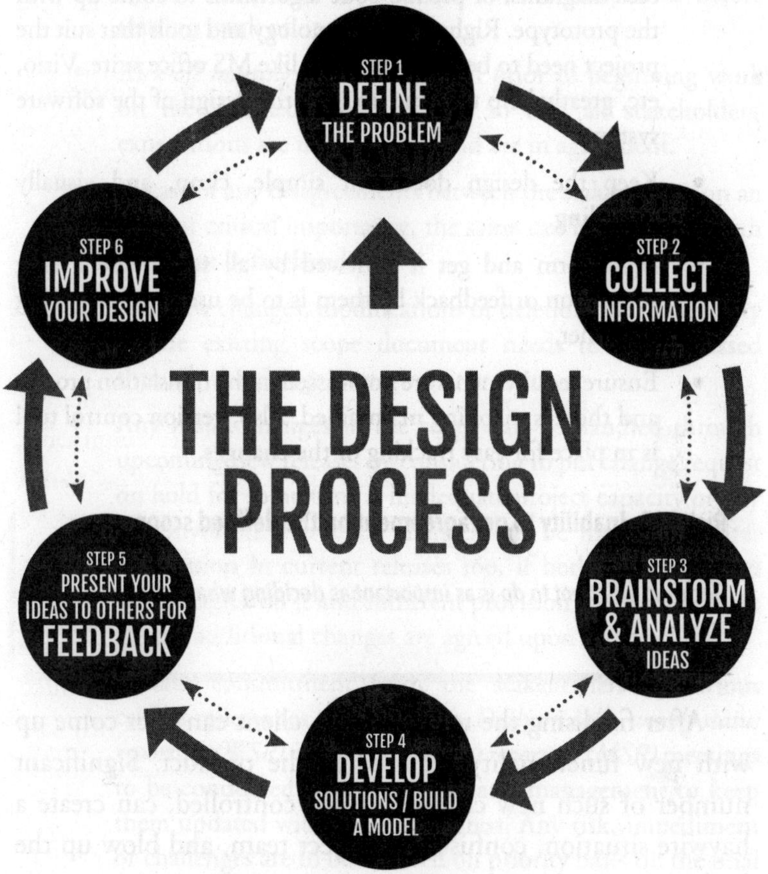

Source discoverdesign.org/handbook

- Get *knowledge transfer* from client *SMEs* who can help you understand the complete picture or go through the product documentation so as to understand it better. Having complete knowledge of problem will help you to easily come up with the technical design of the new or impacted system.

In *scope creep,* also at times known as *requirement creep,* uncontrolled changes are continuously made to the scope by influential stakeholders like client management, sponsors, business users, or vendor management even after the project begins. This is basically due to changes that are made without any proper impact analysis or visualisation of product or service. These create problems later as many other changes are made just to cover up the changes made in earlier stages, thereby starting a chain of changes.

Also, scope creep happens when the scope of product is changed but the project *budget and schedule* remain unchanged.

This issue can occur in a project due to following reasons:-

- ✓ Missed project objectives or objectives not defined properly.
- ✓ Stakeholders failed to visualise the complete product or services which lead to incomplete scope statement.
- ✓ Poor change management process.
- ✓ Poor communication among the stakeholders.
- ✓ Changes in external environment like change in customer preferences, market conditions, industry, regulatory requirements, or technology disruptions.

All these issues in a project ultimately lead to confusion and frustrations of the project team, decreased productivity, high rework, delay in planned schedule, and increase in the costing.

Prevention strategy

- Prepare a solid and complete scope statement considering the holistic view of the product or service.
- Never allow changes to the existing scope without proper analysis and evaluation from business users and sponsor who gave you requirements in the first place.

- Establish a robust *change management system.*
- Establish hierarchy in a project and communication channel between the client and you. Document escalation matrix in a project plan. All internal changes to be controlled by the project manager and leads.
- Promote effective communication among the team members.
- Monitor the project's progress by having regular meetings with all stakeholders periodically—daily, weekly, and monthly, so as to resolve any such issues instantly.

Risk #17–Gold plating issues

Before you 'assume' try this crazy method called 'asking'.

–Anonymous

Gold plating occurs when the programmers and the manager add extra features and functionality in the product that was not requested as part of the scope. These are actually unauthorised changes.

This is generally done by the project team mostly due to assumptions made by them thinking the product lacks something at the moment and this added feature will add value to the product and the client, and also prove their worth to the top management.

Though good sometimes, it often leads to additional cost and increased expectations from the client. Later few functionalities are expected free of cost from your team. Not providing them can make your client dissatisfied.

At times, the newly added functionalities by the developers may not be required by the client and they may reject your product or ask you to rollback the changes done. This may lead to high rework cost and delay in schedule. Also, the product with gold plating may not be saleable in the market as usually the price can be high compared to that of competitor's products.

Prevention strategy

- As a manager, never allow team members to add any extra function or features to the product without proper review or approval from you or the client.
- Establish proper communication lines within the project team.
- Educate the team and newly joined resources about gold plating issues and knowledge of product or application systems they need to develop.
- Peer review of work by the senior resources in a team to be done with the help of a checklist.
- As a project manager monitor the activities of the project on daily basis during status review calls and keep track of the requirements completed, on hold, or in progress by project team members to avoid any unstated requirements.

LEADERSHIP IS THE CAPACITY
TO TRANSLATE
VISION INTO REALITY
—WARREN BENNIS

CHAPTER

03 LEADERSHIP FOCUS

THIS CHAPTER comprises of all the risks or challenges that arise at the top management level with those who are responsible for initiating and controlling the project execution from client or vendor management side.

These risks can occur in a project due to leadership oversight in understanding justification for a proposed project or undertaking on the basis of its expected commercial benefit, capacity and budget management, change in organisation strategy, proposal stage RFP/RFI/RFQ/POC issues, process sacrifices by the senior management, employee engagement, and supplier challenges. The chapter also details the strategies to mitigate the same.

Note: The risks due to oversight of a project team are covered in Chapter 8.

Risk #18–Unjustified or no business case before starting a project

Knowing what you want is the first step towards getting it.

–Mae West

Before formally announcing a project or initiating it, ensure you can justify:-

What benefits it's going to bring to the user of a product or service?

and

Why your company should make an investment in it?

The 'business case' is thus a formal document with justification of a proposed project or undertaking on the basis of expected commercial benefit.

This document comes very handy in the later stages of a project, and helps avoid priority shifts and conflicting thoughts of influential stakeholders—the CEO, sponsors, senior management of the client, and the vendor company by ensuring that the project is worthy of their commitment.

The business case is required for:-

✓ Writing business requirements and ensuring benefits are in agreement with the purpose of investing in the project.

✓ Not having one will lead to weak commitments from stakeholder as motivation of creating some product, adding value to the company or others' life will be missing.

✓ Measuring performance of the senior management by evaluating the feedback from the customer on whether the project delivered the value it was created for.

The above issues of benefits disagreement and weak commitments can even lead to cancellation or keeping the project on hold in the initial or mid phase of the project itself.

Prevention strategy

- Always maintain a well-thought-out business case throughout the execution of the project. It should be unambiguous and clear. Do background research of why you are initiating the project and have clear understanding of the following:-

  ✓ *Gap analysis of the current and future product,* the problem your product is expected to solve for people, organisations, or business users.

- ✓ *Capability and capacity* required in supporting the project which includes human resources, skills, infrastructure, knowledge, and experience needed in a project for developing the product. This also is used to derive the timeframe that will be required for completion of the project with available resources.
- ✓ The *revenue involved*, the expenses required for the project, the profit margin, and return on investment (ROI) expected to be achieved.
- ✓ Whether the project will suit the *mission and vision* for which the company stands.
- ✓ The *opportunity cost* involved.
- ✓ The *risk and opportunity* associated with the project.
- ✓ The *strategic benefits* expected from it like savings in effort, efficiency, learnings from research-based projects, etc.

- The business case to be approved by the sponsor and senior management after which the project can be formally initiated.
- For some reasons, if the project is not able to achieve the expected benefits, document the lessons learnt—what made it fail, and what more could be done better to improve the future products and services. *Some of the thoughts for drafting lessons learnt are:-*
    - ✓ Did the product solve the problem of the users or are we finding some issues while actually using it?
    - ✓ Did we estimate the expected benefits correctly?
    - ✓ Did we develop all the deliverables expected to be planned in business case including the documentation and training material?
    - ✓ Did we develop the right deliverables, or were they lacking something?
    - ✓ Did the technology selected solve the problem faced or were any further problems experienced by the user due to it?
    - ✓ Is the quality of deliverables good and the product easily usable by all?

- ✓ Did something happen internally or externally for not being able to deliver the product expected?
- ✓ What external compliance and internal compliance issues can be held responsible for the failure?

Risk #19–Change in organisation business strategy

People think focus means saying yes to the thing you've got to focus on. But that's not what it means at all. It means saying no to hundred other good ideas that there are. You have to pick carefully.

–Steve Jobs

At times, the priority of your senior vice presidents, department heads or CEO changes as they face day-to-day challenges and their perceptions may change.

At one point in time, they thought that the project was of paramount importance to them and to the organisation, thereby giving you permission as a manager to execute the project; just six months down the line they ask you to cancel the project or put it on hold.

The reasons for this may vary widely, but it could be any of the following:-

- ✓ Due to new opportunities with better outcome than the existing project.
- ✓ Key officials or sponsor may have lost interest in it.
- ✓ Could be the new technology, where they feel existing technology or product is outdated and want to stop it and choose the new one.
- ✓ Lack of funding from the sponsor or the company itself.
- ✓ Dependency constraints from some other teams or third-party issues.
- ✓ Capacity or capability issues of the organisation.
- ✓ Change in organisational strategy like no longer concentrating on manufacturing vertical projects.

✓ All of these may lead to new business priorities or mindset changes that could eventually lead to cancellation of your existing project.

Prevention strategy

- As soon as you, the manager, comes to know of the shift in the sponsor focus or department heads and CEO, arrange meeting with them. Discuss the issue upfront with them, understand the reason for doing so, and try to bring back the focus and their interest in the project. Keep your *business case* handy and discuss with them the benefits the project intends to bring. That's why it is said '*document and keep your project business case handy at all times*' throughout the project duration. And if they request to continue the project again, pursue it till completion.
- If cancellation becomes paramount due to genuine issues, wrap up the project after taking necessary approval from them and other stakeholders. The management needs to talk to the clients and get help of the lawyers in cancelling the project as per procedures laid down in the contract for cancellation of the project. Use arbitration route to settle disputes faster if required.

Risk #20–Failed RFP process or RFP response of low-quality

> ***I was so excited about receiving this RFP, until I started reading it.***
> ***–Anonymous***

Request for Proposal (RFP) is when a client invites bids from different vendors for awarding their project or program for its execution.

Client reviews the bids not only to examine the feasibility, but also the health of the bidding company and the ability of the bidder to actually do what is proposed. Bidders or vendors who have given careful pricing and have a good reputation are selected for asking technicalities before finally signing a contract with them.

Not giving a good response to RFP—not asking right questions or giving right answers, inadequate solution on your part, inappropriate pricing, or not meeting *capacity or capability* needs can cost your organisation hugely by deteriorating your chances of being awarded a multi-million-dollar deal.

Prevention strategy

- Make sure you come to know about the RFPs announced by the customers or client in the first place; connect with the agencies that client employs while announcing new projects and have social presence. Do identify all prospective customers in your area and target market—local, global or specific industry and make sure you are on their radar through appropriate target marketing strategies; reach out to the client companies asking them to be include you in their RFP requests.
- Make sure to get your company name registered with *third party* companies that are engaged by large clients for RFP contract marketing, bidding, and negotiations so as to receive the RFP leads.
- Be proactive. Develop connections, trust, and goodwill with others so as to have insiders who can give you advance tips on the upcoming RFPs.
- *A good response usually should have the following sections:-*
  - ✓ Information about your vendor company.
  - ✓ Specific thoughts on the RFP project and how you are uniquely qualified to succeed.
  - ✓ Your capability, experience, and past project accomplishments.
  - ✓ Answers to the customer's questions.
  - ✓ Your pricing section; and
  - ✓ Your past satisfied client references and testimony.

- RFP response or solution by your organisation should be relevant and detailed with scope, assumptions, high level architecture, tool and technologies, resources, and estimations. Make your response visually appealing, with good graphic images, colour, text, and background.
- Always provide pricing which is bundled, also known as *aggregate pricing* whenever you can. Don't list too many granular details of items as this decreases your chances of better negotiations.
- *Never quote your lowest price*—instead leave room for the customer to 'Win' by giving them around 10 - 12% discount. This way, the customers feel important and associate it with the psychology of 'Win'.
- *Strategically leverage the Q&A process.* As all questions or answers provided by you can be shared with other competing bidders, keep few things secret. At the same time answer the questions which you know will far outshine those of your competitors.
- *Testimonials, referrals, and other support* from past satisfied clients accompanied with good marketing can help to build the image of your company in the mind of the customers and the client company's solicitors. This can greatly help you in being chosen as prospective service provider.
- Use *ready templates for RFP* to save time with standard things applicable to your company and tailored for the same type of project. This ensures 65% things are in place already and 35% things that can be customised as per the individual RFP received.
- Senior managers to *connect with customers* in-person or via online meetings and present the proposal to the client. Any recommendation by the client needs to be addressed by the management. Provide a revised bid if necessary.
- *Have continuous dialogues* with the client's team for building their confidence in your team till official reward of the contract.

Risk #21–Failed proof of concept or low-quality response to your POC or POP

The logic of validation allows us to move between the limits of dogmatism and skepticism.

–Paul Ricoeur

To evaluate if some idea will be feasible or product will meet high priority objectives, *proof of concept (POC)* is used by the customers. This is also an opportunity for the vendor to demonstrate if they are best placed to resolve the current outstanding problems of the client. POC is also known as *proof of principle (POP)*.

Usually, POC is accompanied by demonstration involving small number of stakeholders like sponsor, client management, vendor management, and project team so as to satisfy them whether a prototype developed satisfies certain requirements and solves a given problem. POC does not represent deliverables.

POC or proof of concept is used to avoid failures that could be huge in cost, time or resources, and are often used by client managers before signing contracts with vendors.

Usually, POC fails due to following reasons:-

- ✓ Vendor(s) fail to prove the concept as originally conceived.
- ✓ Concept is working but does not provide the value to the client or other stakeholders.
- ✓ Concept itself was lacking in the first place as few things were not considered.
- ✓ Technology available in the market does not support the concept.

Root cause of above issues can be:-

- ✓ Misunderstood business case or requirements.
- ✓ Lack of executive sponsorship and budget issues.

✓ Lack of vendor team ownership.

✓ Poor *change management process.*

Prevention strategy

- Ensure the selected vendors have required capability, funds, and resources to develop your product. Check their past accomplishments, similar product or service exposure, maximum size, and financial details of projects they successfully delivered in the past, their leader's accomplishments and existing service lines.
- Ensure clear and non-ambiguous business requirements are given by the customer teams to the vendors. The vendor managers and the team need to ask right questions, suggest good solutions, work in parallel with them, so as to build the prototype with permutations and combinations that customer desires from the product. This will help gain customer confidence that vendor knows its job—what to do and how to do it.
- Establish commitments of all the parties that are required to successfully run the POC phase. Seek commitments from the sponsor, business users, and the vendor team for the entire duration of the POC phase. This ensures collaboration is established over cultural boundaries.
- Vendor team and client to select right metrics or *Key Performance Indicators (KPI)* for measuring POC success during the beginning of POC phase itself. Any POC without tangible business benefits at the end is a waste of time and money—and a sure sign that the project would be a failure.
- Select right resources and partners for supporting the POC. Utilise them well.
- Ensure right technology and tools are selected for POC phase.
- Do lots of research before giving demo to clients; develop your presentations with adequate information, right colour, background, fonts, and pictures before delivering actual presentation.

Risk #22–SOW contract legally unenforceable as not signed

Until the contract is signed, nothing is real.

–Glenn Danzig

At times, the SOW contract which is awarded by the client is not signed by their legal authority or by the vendor management due to negligence, lack of knowledge, over-trust or intentionally by the party having maximum risk. This should be avoided at all costs as contracts which are not signed and not registered with legal system are termed *invalid or void contracts* and cannot be presented in a court of law when one of the parties performs in a way that is contrary to the SOW agreement. So, at a later date though *breach of contract* occurs, the party which has done wrong cannot be forced to perform the obligations under the contract, pay penalty, or compensate the amount spent by another party.

Some of the common issues that can occur between the parties are:-

- ✓ Incapacity to deliver as promised in contract.
- ✓ Any conflict related to payments.
- ✓ Scope based problems.
- ✓ Delays in approvals, reporting, shipping products.
- ✓ Failed POC and others.

It is to be noted that some unsigned contracts can be enforced depending upon the way they are drafted, but still it increases the likelihood of costly and time-consuming litigation.

Preventions strategy

- Clear communication in advance by asking the client team executives to sign the contract while awarding it. Unless the contract is signed, work should not be started except under exceptional cases.
- Have some specialised corporate legal advisor draft your contract's terms and conditions, responsibility of parties, and to represent your company.
- Your company's legal internal escalation mechanism for resolving the legal disputes to be put in place. The choice of arbitration route for faster resolution and preference location of jurisdiction can be drafted in the contract itself.
- Client team and your vendor management team to be trained about the impact that an unsigned contract can bring to the organisation and to the client when any conflict or issue occurs while working together or even later in future. All these could cause damage to both the parties' reputation.
- Management and team to do regular follow-ups with the client on periodic basis for signing the contract. However, when there are considerable delays, professional lawyers to be consulted again.

Risk #23–Not assessing the risk related with a contract prior to signing or starting work

Any pitcher you sign to a long-term contract is a risk…you do your homework and make your decision.

–Gerry Hunsicker

Not thoroughly reviewing the contract prior to signing it or beginning work before accepting it can cause issues later in the project. Your SOW resourcing plan might have some critical roles missed, some responsibilities or accountabilities of vendor and client not documented properly, your delivery schedule or milestones may be short and tough on your team. Also, as scope is not known much in the beginning, the actual work could be much more than what appears in the contract and may hit your profit margins.

Apart from these, there might be strict SLA imposed by the client with heavy penalties, the security requirements might be difficult to implement for your company or complexity of work is on higher side.

All these things can bring trouble for your project and company.

Prevention strategy

- Have all your contracts including SOW and MSA read thoroughly by the eminent lawyers or legal team of your company to assess the risks involved.
- Senior managers to assess all the risks in terms of pricing, resourcing, scope, technology, schedule, type of contract, penalties, responsibilities of either party, responsibilities of third party, and type of work.
- Besides this, understand the details of the work at high level, logos and trademarks, titles and subtitles, images provided that can be used in designing or building, but can cause *patent or copyright* issues as per the nature of the project.
- Have formal contract review done as soon as the SOW contract is initiated and finalised, and assess all kinds of risks associated with this new project. Watch out for the political, economic and international change in policies, and your company policies that can bring risk to the project.
- Ensure to discuss such issues with the client and mitigate the risk by putting corrective action thereby renegotiating the deal with the client. If contract brings significant risk to your organisation which cannot be controlled, don't enter into the contract at all with the other party. Rather move on to some other good opportunity available.

Risk #24–Implementing as Big Bang releases rather than as phased releases

How to manage a project? – Limit it in scope. Make it simple. Get success. Then iterate.

–Auren Hoffman

Big Bang releases are one of the major causes of failure. Rather than implementing one big project of one-year duration, implement it incrementally by dividing the scope into portions or bundles of functionalities as short duration releases or series of phases.

Each phase is separated by a decision point known as gates where the criteria for the phase are evaluated by governance before proceeding with the next phase. These five phases could be scoping, creating a business case, product development, testing and validation, and launch.

Example: Implement a large project of 1-year duration by dividing into set of 4 phases or releases of 3 months each followed by its review at each phase.

Implementing a project this way increases focus of a team on each set of functionalities of a product in every release and gives them sense of achievement on completion of minor milestone every time. This leads to high performance and better deliverables at every phase. Also, regular feedback from client reduces risk and impediments, establishes better commitments from team, increases collaboration and clarity in achieving a great quality product rather than customer knowing that the product is substandard only after a year. Thus, releasing a project in incremental or series of phases, often termed as *phase-gate process or stage-gate process* releases tends to reduce risk and cost.

Prevention strategy

- Divide your project into multiple releases through *phase-gate process* rather than implementing as single release. Each release to have a stack of multiple functionalities that can be implemented together.
- Ensure thorough review at each decision point or gate and plan for the next phase.
- You can adopt result focused approach—*Agile* methodology or other models like *Spiral* to build your product this way.

Agile based methodology features are listed below:-

✓ Divides your work or application system to be developed into user stories and develops them in small iterations called *sprints* (often of 2 weeks' duration).

✓ Greatly increases the control of client management through regular feedback at the end of each sprint and also on daily basis with scrum teams comprising developer, tester, etc.

✓ Retrospective meeting is held at the end of each sprint to measure 'what went well', 'what did not' and 'what can be improved.'

✓ Greatly reduces the surprises that customer gets to see at the end of the waterfall model projects after long interval, as risks are managed every day via sprint calls.

✓ Deployment of components can be done on regular basis within the sprints or can be postponed for later set of sprints, after measuring the impact that can happen on implementing a portion of the product in live environment.

Risk #25–Excessive product quality sacrifices by senior management

Quality is always the result of excellent work without compromise.

–Anonymous

In business, there are incidents when the senior management or the CEO may fear losing market share to rivals. This can be due to their organisation lacking a product to compete with in particular segment or competitor has come up with an innovative product that existing products in the market cannot match.

Example: **A leading international China-based mobile company launched an innovative smartphone at mouth-watering price with all best features for middle-class section of society, and your company XYZ's mobile products are failing to compete with it. Moreover, you lack the kind of technology, capability, and supplier advantage of providing high-tech mobile parts in large volumes and at low price. The final price thus offered by China-based competitor is much lower and something which your company XYZ cannot match at the moment with the available resources.**

As a result, all customers are buying the high-tech competitor product and your mobile company fears loss of market share due to its inability to perform in particular segment or market.

The board of directors of company XYZ, due to this competitive pressure, may demand from the CEO to create similar smartphone but at a price lower or nearly at the same level. As a result, the vendor team, due to this urgency, may come up with a smartphone product having similar aesthetic features of competitor products, but of poor-quality, lacking in performance and reliability. The primary reason is because the management and team parted with many quality checks, processes, and used cheap mobile parts to reduce the final price.

The above strategy may work sometimes in terms of saving market share, but may prove costly for the company in long run—when customers start complaining about the product, bad-mouth it publicly through social media or other medium. This eventually results in loss of trust from customers and them parting ways permanently.

Prevention strategy

- Senior management and other stakeholders should weigh the features desired in the product against the cost. Prioritisation techniques discussed in Risk #12 to be considered. Using these techniques, a useful product with limited features can still be developed without compromising on quality.
- Ensure all the important processes and quality standards recommended as a part of ISO 9000, CMMI, Six Sigma, COBIT 5, etc. are in place as per the nature of project and none of the process steps are taken for granted.
- Ensure proper verification system and review in place at every important stage in a product lifecycle using thorough review checklist during requirements, design, testing and implementation. Ensure sufficient review effort—say 10% of the normal effort to be spent on each phase.
- Carefully examine the quality of the product with the help of dedicated quality assurance testers, taking note of internal defects during testing.
- Ensure defect management system tool is in place where all internal and customer defects are logged and analysed. Any suggestions by stakeholders to be incorporated in the product before going for final release into production.
- Ensure *sign-off process* from the influential stakeholders are in place, once significant stages like design, testing, and implementation are completed.
- Training managers and team on the importance of quality

process, defect management, and quality standard is a must. Spreading quality culture is what company should strive for.

- Timely audit by internal and external auditors to be scheduled and lapses observed to be closed by the project manager on priority.

Risk #26–Not investing in company-wide improvement initiatives

Continual improvement is an unending journey.

–Lloyd Dobyns

A company, if not taking due care to improve *processes* day by day is sure-shot on a path to failure. To remain in business, you need to keep on improving day in and day out in everything you do, as your best practice.

Not monitoring and measuring what you do and not working on the improvement will always lead to dissatisfied customer or client due to outdated ways of doing things. This will never allow you to build great quality products or services and can get you out of the business in quick time.

Prevention strategy

- Invest in improvement initiatives of your company, set up quality department and hire the best internal audit consultants. Get your projects audited by them. They will do internal audits of your projects as independent party and ensure high performance is achieved.
- Ensure the *quality management system (QMS)* of your company is drafted as per the latest ISO 9000, CMMI guidelines, standards and best practices, and all the processes followed by projects in various departments are defined in your company's QMS. Your project manager and team should adhere to these processes while conducting their projects and address the gaps found by auditors. Manager

and team to close gaps found in audit and ensure continual improvement in process and delivery.

- Invest in setting up independent quality assurance teams like team of independent testers for carrying verification and validation of projects without notice on adhoc basis. Such a team should verify the products in terms of meeting the functionalities as given in the requirements. This will ensure clients or customers receive world-class products or services from your organisation.
- Top management to review *balanced scorecard (BSC)* and associated reports from financial, customer, internal process, and organisational capacity viewpoint and take necessary actions to improve things.

Risk #27–Not able to fulfill resource demands when actual opportunity knocks

or

Optimistic resource assumptions

Opportunity dances with those already on the dance floor.

–H Jackson Brown, Jr

A project can be at risk of failing to deliver due to *inadequate number of resources or less skilled resources* in a team which puts quality and schedule of a project in jeopardy. *These can be due to:-*

- ✓ Senior managers have other priority projects that may put your project on the backburner. So, when your project actually starts, there might not be adequate resources to meet your project needs.
- ✓ The organisation buffer resource pool strength might be inadequate leading to lost opportunity—as organisation may fail to fulfill positions demanded by the client on time.
- ✓ Also, at times, highly optimistic resource estimates are done

for a project by senior management thinking key resources are 100% committed to the project, while in reality they have other personal commitments.

✓ Team may have inadequate skilled resources due to lack of experience, knowledge, or right attitude as hiring process in a company went wrong in the first place.

Prevention strategy

- Make sure to negotiate with your senior managers by detailing them on the commitments that the client seeks from the vendor on human resources and pitch the benefits that the project is going to bring. Ensure to highlight the disadvantages—bad reputation and business loss for the company by not committing to this project.
- Gain budget from department heads and create a staffing plan with adequate resources and needs.
- Do advance hiring by getting in touch with your company HR; hire few more resources than actually needed that can be used as buffers in crises situations or when there is increase in project resource demand over the tenure of the project.
- Check with other project managers for negotiation of top high-skilled performers with exposure in relevant domain, application, and technical skills. This is required in your project for fulfilling lead positions so as to maintain a balanced competitive team.
- Hire resources with different skills and experience composition—some with expertise in one desired technology and tools, while others in alternative technology or tools; some good in domain or business skills, while others in developing and testing the project deliverable. Make these resources teach other resources and promote cross-skilling which will help in forming a competitive team.
- Prior to actual initiation of a project, manager to have one-on-one meeting with the applicants and ask for their

commitment till the duration of the project, as listed in the contract. If any risk is foreseen post discussion with the candidate, like *lack of commitment* which can arise due to behavioural attitude problems or other plans like marriage, maternity leave, higher education leaves, then probably you need to look for other resource as alternative. Often, these are reasons that lead to delay in meeting project schedule or poor team performance later in a project when replacement of a resource is not available in quick time.

Risk #28–Inability of vendor to execute project due to capability limitations

Consistent alignment of capabilities and internal processes with the customer value proposition is the core of any strategy execution.

–Robert S Kaplan

Let's say your vendor management bid for a project and won it. Soon, they realise they are unable to fill some significant positions with desired skill sets and experience required as per the contract.

Example**: The company HR failed to provide 1 Business analyst in domain property-casualty line and 3 Technical experts in new technologies like Big data and Salesforce required as per the project contract.**

On top of it, deadline for a project initiation is nearing. Waiting further is not an option, as you may fall behind schedule, and end up eating the funds allocated by the client for the same, and hamper your reputation.

Here are few other instances of capability risk and why it is a prominent risk for vendors when it comes to managing any projects:-

Case 1: **A resource in a company knew about the application better than others. When he left, the project collapsed as the other team members lacked knowledge about the same.**

Case 2: **A manager hired from top B-School was excellent and knew how to select suppliers. However, when he resigned the new manager faced lot of issues and took a lot of time aligning with the other departmental managers.**

Capability is the driving force of an organisation and cannot be acquired by spending money on them immediately. Capabilities are intangible assets of an organisation and it means having edge over competitors in processes, technologies, and knowledge.

Prevention strategy

- Prior to entering into proposals like RFP, ensure you have resources with required skill set and necessary infrastructure to support the same.
- Analyse the risks and check if you can outsource the risky portion of the scope to third parties and share revenue. Monitor the work of third-party vendor and their quality practices and processes on periodic basis
- Look to hire contracted employees by consulting the recruiters in the market who can provide you with skilled resources immediately.
- Understand customer's current and future demands for services and produce forecasts for future requirements. This helps you to plan your resources well in advance for successfully completing the projects
- Project team to maintain repository of tools, documentation of application, and best practices. Management to ensure that the resources are skilled to carry out project activities at all times.

- Take steps to improve existing processes. Document them in QMS.
- Automation and reusability to be given special focus as these greatly increase your efficiency in doing work. Invest in technology and tools that will help you to gain competitive advantage.
- Hiring the resources in advance for the company, fostering up-skilling of resources through training, cross-skilling of resources, and establishing great cultural environment will always ensure that you have a pool of capable resources available at all times to take up challenging roles.

Risk #29–Struggling with cost management

A budget is telling your money where to go instead of wondering where it went.

–Dave Ramsey

Your project may no longer be profitable for your company. Perhaps it was poorly run as proper planning and execution was not done properly or the right processes were not in place which caused the trouble. Probably some defect fixing took lot of time or its pre-sales team did not pitch right. Often, it could be lack of knowledge and experience of team and improper technology selected that has put the project in jeopardy.

Whatever is the case, issues like the ones highlighted above have led to extended schedule and budget allocated has gone for a toss. Your project has become a pain now and it's on the verge of failure due to shortage of funds.

Prevention strategy

- Monitor the spending on the project on daily basis before it succumbs to massive cost overruns. Track the spending on daily basis using charts and tools. Plan the project budget.

Plan for contingency factor in estimates due to things outside your control like resources, expected delays in financing, market cycles, product or service supply shortages, exchange rate fluctuations, etc. Regularly revisit the resource forecast, record timesheets of resources, eliminate scope creep, and always keep the stakeholders informed of the budget spending and actions to keep it under control.

- Have regular status review calls on a daily or weekly basis with all stakeholders—any bottlenecks, risk or issues to be addressed upfront and timely actions to be taken to mitigate them.
- Senior management to analyse the budgetary issues in the project and understand the root cause of the issue by discussing with the project manager. They need to discuss with the client too and note their feedback. Once this is done, take necessary actions to address the issues.
- Utilise the critical path method to figure out the critical tasks pending. Utilise your resources effectively to complete these without any delay and other activities in parallel with them. Infuse more resources if need arises or ask team to work for some extra hours and meet this schedule. Consider changing the resource's responsibility if you are not getting good output from the current allocated resource.
- Get your project audited internally or seek help externally from quality consulting firms in the market and introduce measures to improve processes as part of corrective action.
- Prepare the lessons learnt from such failure to prevent such issues in future.

Risk #30–Not doing resource capacity planning properly

A learning organisation is an organisation that is continually expanding its capacity to create its future.

–Peter Senge

Capacity planning in project management ensures—provision of resources with necessary skills at all times and resources are skilled enough to implement strategically relevant projects at right time. It is the process of matching the work to be done with the available resources, where resources can be people, infrastructure, machines, or others.

In order to effectively deliver the project deliverables on time with high quality in limited budget and with high profit margin, the managers need to effectively utilise the resources in a project. These resources should be experienced and skilled enough to deliver the products and services which are required in the market.

Also, in a given *portfolio*—set of projects with related outcome of particular account or service area, the managers need to effectively allocate the limited resources in these projects to achieve the maximum revenue and profit margin. The same measures need to be realised at the organisation level as well.

Prevention strategy

- Maintain the list of limited resources along with their skill sets, start date of allocation in given projects, ending of assignments with the particular projects, their rate card, location, and other details in a tool. Have a dedicated portfolio manager who can coordinate with HR managers to fulfill resource demands and utilise resources effectively in projects.
- A project manager needs to assign right resources to a particular task based on skill set and expertise so as to meet the milestone schedules and complete project on time. He/she needs to effectively allocate the resources as per work breakdown structure (WBS) to tasks in critical path. This will ensure capacities are matched with requirements. Also

ensure that other adhoc activities that go on in a project are also managed without affecting the core project activities.

- Manager should also consider the releases planned within a given period, say weekly or monthly, and allocate the resources as per their availability. Also, have a backup planned in case someone is on leave, which will require adequate capacity planning on your side and sufficient buffer resources to take care of activities without impacting the deliveries in absence of responsible team members.
- Keep a tool to track the skills of each of the resources and any skill gap that may arise with respect to the nature of the work. Conduct regular training of the resources to upskill them by teaching additional skills and cross-train them for sharing different job responsibilities in a project.
- When managing portfolio, ensure to have details logged in a tool about each unique project like project name, start date, end date, type of project, project manager, sponsor, resource requirement, and its RGY (Red, Green, Yellow) status reflecting the current control or state of the project. Observe dependency between them, prioritise appropriately and also identify unimportant projects which can be postponed, if need arises.
- Avoid resource conflict in a project and create an environment in which everyone treats each other with respect. Establish a culture where everyone is appreciated and empowered in the company.

Risk #31–Not driving periodic review with project team by the senior management

or

Lack of project visibility

Review your goals twice every day in order to be focused on achieving them.

–Les Brown

Statistically it has been proven that greater the control senior management or client exercises over the project activities through periodic status review, the lesser are the chances of projects failing to attain their objectives.

This happens due to variety of factors like better periodic feedbacks, mitigation of risk on regular basis before final product gets ready, driving improvements in the project, and better commitments from the team and management that leads to less confusion, more clarity, and better delivery.

Prevention strategy

- Have regular periodic meetings—daily, weekly, biweekly or monthly with client, senior management, and team to discuss work progress, improvements, and initiatives.
- Ensure senior managers discuss the risks and issues in the project with the project managers and team thereby closely monitoring and guiding them.
- Ensure necessary support is provided to the managers and their team on matters of resources, infrastructure, finance thereby coordinating with other departments like HR, finance, and admin team for faster approval and support.
- Use well-structured ready templates for presentations during review calls covering all process areas, KPIs, delivery progress, risk and issues, resourcing, and work planned in future as this enables better monitoring and control.

Risk #32–Employee engagement and satisfaction not getting measured

To win in the market place you must first win in the workplace.

–Douglas Conant

The greatest asset of a company is its employees. A smart CEO and business leader should not only measure the customer satisfaction of a project, but also ensure satisfaction of the human resources committed to it.

A good project manager and senior management can help the CEO in a great way in this mission by encouraging the resources they work with on daily basis. It is rightly said—'*a company is only as good as the management team it hires*'. So, when management fails to take care of the needs of the resources, it indicates failure of an organisation too.

Prevention strategy

- Regular meetings and discussions should be done with the team members of the project and their feedback on improvement they seek in a project, its work environment, or organisation culture to be taken care of. This includes aligning career goals with their aspirations and even helping them out during some major family crises.
- Once management takes note of these issues, they should in their capacity help to resolve these issues by taking appropriate actions.
- Regular appreciations, acknowledgements, and feedback to be provided for every employee who achieves something in the project by the managers and the client.
- Performance review and employee appraisal system adopted should be fair. Project team members exhibiting good knowledge and performance should be given better rating than others. Better career opportunities to be given to such high performers. It's now an accepted fact that employees who stay late most of the times are given better rating, but it should be otherwise—employees who achieve better results in the regular 9 hours of office work should be rewarded better. Performance achieved, knowledge exhibited, and

results produced should be given preference.

- Develop sound and impartial HR policy for appraisal system, awards and rewards, reimbursement, compensation, release from organisation, anti-harassment, dress code, travel, loans, and extra hour's compensation. Also, employees' code of conduct guidelines to be drafted by company and followed by every employee. This creates a culture of trust and respect in organisation and avoids conflict.
- Promote vacation time for your employees. This helps them to unwind and could boost their productivity which is actually good for the organisation. However, this needs to be planned. Make your workplace relaxed; nobody likes to work in a serious environment. Be approachable; delegate more than just work, and abolish hierarchy system, at times that is the best solution.

Risk #33–Poor supplier management

In a very real sense, there are only two roles in organisations: customers and suppliers. Everybody functions simultaneously in both roles, whether inside or outside the organisation the essence of good business therefore is the quality of relationship between customer and supplier.

–Stephen Covey

Your company depends on the services of third parties like suppliers for the software, computers, laptops, network, seating arrangements, salary processing of its employees, legal chartered accountant's services for financial reporting, taxation, etc.

Issues with supplier (or vendor) can happen any time during the period of contract with relations going sour which can turn out to be very frustrating and costly affair for the service provider and the clients. This can cause project to deviate from its objectives.

Prevention strategy

- Create *vendor selection criteria* to reduce bias and malpractices. Vendor's product or service offering, prior experience, satisfied client list, costing, security needs, and brand name are some parameters to be considered before selecting them as a partner and entering into contract.
- Create the bid documents to summarise your organisation's needs and your criteria. *Three most common types of bid documents are:-*
  - ✓ *RFI (Request for Information)*—is used where the customer needs more information, not only the price of products or services. It's mostly used for internal planning. Mostly RFI is followed by RFQ or RFP.
  - ✓ *RFQ (Request for Quote) or (Invitation for Bid)*—generally used when the customer is primarily looking for price quotations. It is standard business process used to invite suppliers into bidding process on specific products or services.
  - ✓ *RFP (Request for Proposal)*—document describing a business problem or need and asking for the vendors to propose a solution.
- Proposals received are then evaluated for selecting the final supplier from the list of two or three suppliers shortlisted from the proposals' list. Do negotiate before signing the deal with the final supplier and choose one whose commitment is of highest level.
- Manage the supplier relationship by setting clear expectations with them and monitor their performance through regular status review calls. Identify the *key performance indicators (KPIs)* that will be used for measuring the vendor success and place penalty and rewards to bring focus and commitment of the vendor. Report and highlight the issues to the vendor management for improvement.
- Over a period of time or at the time of renewal, reflect on whether you want to continue with the vendor or end the contract due to substandard services and make it open for another supplier. To exercise this option, ensure that you have a provision in the contract drafted for the formalities required during such closures.

THE REAL PROBLEM IS
NOT WHETHER MACHINES
THINK
BUT WHETHER MEN DO.
—BF SKINNER

CHAPTER 04 TECHNOLOGY AND TOOLS SELECTION

TECHNOLOGY AND tools facilitate in achieving desired outcome of the project as per the contract and help to solve real-world problems. Selecting the right set of technologies and tools for a project is therefore paramount. This chapter explores various risks associated with them that can put your project in jeopardy.

Risk #34–Unforeseen technology dependencies

Technology presumes there's just one right way to do things and there never is.

–Robert M Pirsig

Technology and tools selected should be appropriate for the development of the product.

Every technology has certain positive and negative aspects that need to be assessed before choosing them for product development or services.

Let's consider the case of *Java* technology. Java has advantages—the apps developed are easily portable on any platform, gives more liberty in choosing whatever operating system you want for production and development, are backward compatible and migration between different Java platforms is smooth. At the same time, Java GUI is efficient making it a preferred choice for creating app interface. However, disadvantages associated include its susceptibility to security breaches since it is platform independent. Also, since it supports multi-platform, Java programs can run slower than others, and also require more memory space.

.Net on the other hand, is a preferred choice to design applications for specific business functions such as finance, CRM, and supply management as it provides scalability which allows re-designing applications to serve growing needs of an organisation later. It allows the entire range of computing devices to work together, and helps integrate various communication media such as e-mail, fax, and phones. It has disadvantages too as migrating applications to .NET can be expensive, involves a vendor lock-in, thereby making future development solely dependent on Microsoft managed code and can be slower than native code.

Similarly, others like *Big data, Salesforce* have some advantages and disadvantages that you need to consider before you choose them.

Also, technology like *Mainframe* has lost its relevance, but is still used today by giant corporations like American Express, AmerisourceBergen, etc. This is due to overhead and heavy cost associated with migrating to new applications, it's relatively virus free, and provides great speed when it comes to processing data of millions of customers.

Not selecting a particular technology based on the product's needs and client's expectation may lead to major rework and delay in project. Moreover, the product developed may become obsolete with time easily and future maintenance can become a costly affair.

Prevention strategy

- *Some of the things that you can consider when selecting right tool and technology are:-*
  - ✓ size of data your system is going to process,
  - ✓ whether the product will be used online or offline,
  - ✓ processing needs and performance requirement,
  - ✓ maintainability,
  - ✓ scalability needs like number of users that can be supported at a time,
  - ✓ other application system it will integrate with,
  - ✓ operating system it can work with and features that it will support,
  - ✓ long term vendor support.
- Consider collaborating with technical experts or an external agency that has worked in similar technologies.
- Come up with an adequate impact analysis report detailing the technology changes involved in the impacted or new system.
- Consider your application dependency with upstream systems and downstream systems; their technology, database, and architecture need before choosing some technology for your application as overall performance may suffer. Brainstorm with impacted application team's directors or architects for new changes and technology that will suit them best and why.
- Other significant factors that can influence enterprises in their choice of technology are—their comfort zone in some skills and expertise, existing skills, infrastructure, cost of development, spending involved in purchasing some new software and tools, and complexity of application to be developed.
- The technology selected finally should be documented as part of the scope with justification for its selection, the

competitive edge it offers, better processing and performance edge it will give to your customers that no other technology can give. This document should be signed and approved by clients while awarding the contract to the vendors.

- At times, the *proof of concepts (POC)* phase can be run to understand the feasibility of given idea by developing some prototype with technology in question, testing it, and only then proceeding further for full application development.

Risk #35–Security vulnerabilities in chosen technology and product

For every lock there is someone out there trying to pick it or break in.
–David Bernstein

Security vulnerabilities in a chosen technology due to weakness in system security procedures, design, internal controls, and administrative controls can trigger unforeseen risks from virus, worms, and hackers' attacks, that can corrupt the computer, disk, systems, and other devices. These can lead to loss of data, rework, and deviation from schedule ultimately leading to increase in the project cost.

Moreover, security issues in existing product can make it obsolete in quick time when customer software system gets corrupted or is hacked. It eventually leads to decrease in demand of your product and reduction in market share due to adverse publicity received.

Such non-compliance in security aspects can bring legal lawsuits against your company by client or other parties that can prove to be very costly and time-consuming affair.

Prevention strategy

- Carefully evaluate your technology and tools selection

criteria considering the security aspects of the technology—confidentiality, integrity, and availability (CIA) while designing architecture of software system. Some other factors to consider are layers of protection it's going to offer, the security features it's going to support, information characteristics of data, the database and software systems it integrates with, and the hardware and operating system required for its running.

- Consult software security experts, architects, hackers and business users who can expose vulnerabilities in existing product, and help to choose the right technology. Managers should even do brainstorming with all the stakeholders before going ahead with a particular technology.
- Choose firewall, security software, antivirus tools, long passwords, fingerprint scanners, and face detection tools that can protect your system applications data and product from attacks outside the networks.
- Ensure security related test cases are comprehensive, covering all internal and external aspects of software and thorough testing is done, thereby producing a product which is both robust and secure. Never fail to consider the aspects of environment in which the software is going to run.
- Ensure that all partners and stakeholders are onboard in the project after thorough background screening checks.
- Educate your staff on security aspects such that it becomes a part of company culture.

Risk #36–Outdated technology or tool selection

Any sufficiently advanced technology is equivalent to magic.

–Sir Arthur C Clarke

Sometimes, the client or customer asking for development of some product from vendor may select outdated technology, simply because they fail to notice that the market and customer preferences have changed or they may have inadequate knowledge on certain aspects of technology and tools.

Also, it may happen that the existing product or application system is making use of technology like Mainframe-DB2 which is too old now and its existing customers do not find convenience in using it. Moreover, the response time in using these applications can be on the higher side causing performance issues. This eventually leads to customers switching to competitor products using modern efficient technologies like .NET and Oracle.

Issues like above can affect your existing or future IT business, leading to lower profit margin for your company due to decline in sales or performance of your application system.

Prevention strategy

- Management and team to analyse customer requirements, educate the client and suggest to them the disadvantages of using outdated technologies. The team can help the client with best technology and tools suited for their requirements or application and justify the advantages of using alternate available new technologies—the benefits it brings in terms of better processing speed, user interface, memory management, security, scalability, and performance.
- Team can demonstrate past completed projects, testimonies of previous customers, and current market trends to suggest the client to switch to a new technology.
- Upgradation or replacement of the existing outdated software and tools needs to be done after taking approval from the senior management. Migration of certain legacy application to new application with better technology

support emerges as the need of the hour. For example—Mainframe-DB2 application to .Net and Oracle.

- Senior management and project team to keep a tab on the technology disruptions taking place in the market and ensure foolproof strategy to counter its effects or adopt it for betterment of services and customer satisfaction.

Risk #37–Lack of tools to capture internal defect and effort spent on project activities

In a true zero-defect approach, there are no unimportant items.

–Phil Crosby

There should be separate software tool for logging and monitoring the internal defects as it is not desirable for internal defects to be known to the client, as this can alienate the client.

Team also needs to log the effort and time spent on project activities, rework, and fixing defects. These internal defects need to be analysed by the project managers periodically as they give clues of the issues in the project and highlight weak areas of project management.

Prevention strategy

- All the tasks in the project are to be planned by the team. The effort spent on them, the internal defects, and the review effort spent on these activities should be tracked as part of the project management activities.
- *Defect description, detection phase, occurrence phase, severity of defects, and causes of the defects* are some parameters in *defect management* tools that need to be captured. In addition, effort spent on fixing these defects should also be captured.
- This data can be analysed from time to time by the managers to understand the *root cause* of these defects. Generally, *Pareto* analysis chart technique is used to identify the root

causes of defects in the industry. Statistically, 80% of the defects are due to 20% of the root causes found as per the widely accepted management principle *80/20 rule*. These 20% root causes can be due to various engineering issues and must be analysed for improvements by incorporating a corrective action in place.

- Besides the above mentioned, project data is used by independent auditors for giving feedback in project management areas that need improvement. Such areas to be corrected by having right action plan in place, measuring, and monitoring them till successful closure.

Risk #38–Lack of tools to capture defects detected by the customers

The zero-defect principle says: 'Do it right the first time.'

–Philip Crosby

Not having customer defect logging tool will not allow you or your client to have correct picture of the defect and quality of delivery met by your organisation.

Having such tools gives the number of defects leaked to customers at any stage in product development or maintenance services. This helps to gauge the quality issues that the project is faced with in different stages. The tracking becomes easy which ensures all the customer defects are closed on time by intimating the person responsible for them.

This is very useful in multi-vendor projects as each vendor team is able to figure out the defects and issues they need to take care of—at the same time the customer knows which vendor has done a better job.

Prevention strategy

- Check with the client for having tool where customer defects can be logged, so as to ascertain the delivery quality.

- Defect management tools available in the market like *HP Quality Center*, *JIRA* can be utilised by the project team after taking approval from the client. Agile management tools like *Rally* and *VersionOne* also allow defects to be tracked. So, if you are using any one of these, there's no need to purchase any other tool.
- If customer defect logging tool is not provided in your project, talk to your management and check whether such a tool can be introduced in the project. Consider developing in-house tools, if need arises.
- If no customer defect logging tool is allowed by the client, the team can use Microsoft Excel or any other tool to maintain customer defects and track them with visibility to the client. They can also be tracked using internal defect and effort logging tools provided by your organisation itself.
- The defect metrics and issues to be discussed in defect prevention meetings, and corrective actions to be considered for improving things further, after their root cause analysis.

Risk #39–Insufficient tools in the project for working efficiently

> ***Losing is inevitable, make sure you have the tools in your toolbox to deal with it.***
>
> ***–Rich Franklin***

This is another reason which can put the project in jeopardy or delay the delivery. Tools are mostly provided by the client in projects, but your organisation should have repository of all the major tools that are required to provide business solutions.

Similarly, many other tools are required for the project management activities—testing, debugging, costing, internal reporting, analysis, designing, implementation, and automation activities, so as to ease the job in hand and work more efficiently.

Example:

a) **Your project may need *Microsoft Excel* tool for doing analysis on the data. Apart from these, tools like *HP Quality Center* is required for logging and tracking defects.**
b) **The project may require *Rally* or *VersionOne* tool to manage your Agile projects' user stories, acceptance criteria, estimation, deliverables tracking, burndown charts, burnup charts, and status tracking for each user stories.**

Prevention strategy

- Tools provided by the client for carrying project activities to be carefully evaluated for sufficiency by planning a meeting of all the stakeholders including client at the initiation stage of project itself. All the necessary tools that are needed by the team for project completion to be discussed. Team can later suggest to client to provide any missing tools. This practise helps greatly.
- Ensure consistency of tools among the key stakeholders. This helps in effective coordination between different teams.
- Team to bring to the notice of the project manager any additional tool that could be required over period of time by giving proper justification of the benefits the tool brings and significant saving achieved in effort, cost, time, or convenience.
- Management to discuss with the client the benefits of the tool. However, if the client is not ready to provide the tool due to costing or other issues, the vendors themselves can look to purchase and provide their project team the desired tools. This option to be exercised only when benefits outweigh the costs involved and the client has no problem with this new tool's usage.
- Your organisation itself can fund development of such tools in-house but don't forget to showcase this as a value addition activity to your client.

- Often, multiple tools are available in the market for similar purpose due to which it can become a complex decision for your team to identify which tool would be better than the others. For such critical decisions, evaluate the alternative tools based on parameters of success like performance, effort, usability, cost of purchase, reliability, and only then choose the final tool.

Risk #40–Poor configuration management practices and tools

It is not the strongest or the most intelligent who will survive but those who can best manage change.

–Charles Darwin

Configuration management (CM) is a mandatory process required as a part of CMMI recommendations for *maintaining service assets of projects and controlling changes throughout the lifecycle of a project*. It is often a snapshot of the entire system building blocks.

CM tools allow only single user to make changes in the program or other component at a time and ensures correct version is used by the resources for modification each time. This is very useful when there are a lot of stakeholders who have access to the assets and can tamper with them. These tools maintain a log of activities when making any alterations to the assets which helps to identify the one who might have tampered with it.

Some of the advantages it provides are:-

- ✓ Helps to know the current state of the system. This helps in easy restoration of service when any security breach or tampering by the other stakeholders.
- ✓ Better control over process activities.
- ✓ Avoids duplication of assets and confusion of the resources.
- ✓ Cost reduction.

✓ Useful in change management process.

Prevention strategy

- CM planning to be done at the start of the project and all the tools required for this to be identified by the stakeholders. Dedicated shared folders or tools for keeping artifacts to be planned.
- Crucial assets of the project that require control of changes to be identified—SOPs (standard operating procedures), programs, design, test case artifacts etc. Ensure these have controlled access as per the roles in the project. Reviewers to be defined for baselining these artifacts.
- CM tools like SVN, ChangeMan, or TFS that are readily available in the market can be purchased and used. Team can also create in-house tool if costing is not an issue.
- If defects have occurred due to CM activities, the same need to be analysed and corrective actions to be put in place, and monitored till successful closure.
- CM internal and external audits can be scheduled on periodic basis, so as to identify gaps in the process. The corrective actions needs to be monitored and closed by the project manager on time.

{ THE CLIENT MAY BE KING,
BUT HE'S NOT
THE ART DIRECTOR.
—VON GLITSCHKA }

CHAPTER

05 CHALLENGES AT CUSTOMER/CLIENT END

SENIOR MANAGEMENT or the project team is not responsible for all the risks. There are other risks or challenges that occur due to the client/customer management team's lack of knowledge on processes, cultural differences with vendors, changes in client management team, inability to support the vendor team on time, funding issues by the sponsors, and not receiving customer feedback on time. This chapter explores many such risks and strategies to mitigate these.

Risk #41–Process sacrifices by client

People that aren't used to quality always chase quantity.

–Anonymous

Often process sacrifices are made by the client team, and this is one of the most significant reasons for failure of many projects in the real world.

This can happen due to any of the following reasons:-

- ✓ Clients may lack maturity or knowledge and would not want to review and provide official sign-off or acceptance on some of the significant intermediate deliverables like on finalised requirements, design, or test case review provided by the vendors as they might think that it is a risk. As a result, the project team may lack guidance and lose commitment.

- ✓ Often, the client may over-trust the vendor due to the long-term business relationship between them and would not like to have control over the day-to-day operations.
- ✓ Sometimes, the clients are new in the outsourcing business and may lack knowledge on quality process to be established, service level agreement (SLA) or operation control they need to exercise on the vendor. In such cases, a lot depends on the vendor managers and their technical team's competency. Any lack in commitments or knowledge by the project team can lead to the failure of the projects.
- ✓ At times, clients do this to save time for faster delivery and execution, due to responsibility and accountability issues within their team—limited team size, due to negligence, and past ways of doing things from a long time.
- ✓ Also, due to overconfidence and beliefs where they thought that skipping some process would still give them the final results they wanted.

Prevention strategy

- As a project manager, ensure you have all applicable processes in place as per the latest global standards of ISO, CMMI process models, COBIT etc. considering the nature of your project.
- Check SOW contract for processes to be followed in the project and discuss with client for any anomaly. Ensure that the client takes due care in establishing all client involving processes like sign-off on requirements, estimations, design, test cases, and provides the feedback on successful implementation.
- Monitor and measure your processes and improve them further.
- Make sure your projects get audited by internal or external auditor. Any lapses in process found during audit which are not justified, need to be checked with the client team and necessary changes in processes to be incorporated

as improvement initiative. If customer is not convinced or feels that some process can be skipped while auditor and management feel it can cause a risk, the same can be documented as risk in the project risk tracker and monitored.

- Have regular review calls with the client, project team, and quality assurance team. Discuss project activity status and improvements to understand what more can be done for better results.
- As a manager always consider inputs from your project team for improvement in process and service delivery. Develop the culture of quality in your project and as someone rightly said *'Quality is a habit not an act'*. So, instill it as a habit in all your team members.

Risk #42–No clear development methodology identified during project initiation

The methodology is similar to a cooking recipe. The recipe tells you how to cook a meal while software development methodologies tell you how to build a software product.

–Ritesh Mehta

Your choice of a methodology determines how your team is going to work and communicate with the stakeholders to achieve better end results. There are various software methodologies prescribed for developing a software product like waterfall, agile, iterative, incremental, v-model, rapid application development (RAD), etc. Every methodology has certain advantages and disadvantages. Selection of the right one depends on your project objective and resources available at your disposal.

Not selecting right methodology will lead to confusion as your team will end up missing or repeating activities leading to a lot of bugs in a software product and eating up the budget allocated by the client or your department.

Prevention strategy

- If methodology is not selected by the client during SOW contract or within one week after project starts, vendor management to work with the client, and suggest appropriate methodology as per the nature of the project and client needs.

  Some of the criteria that can be used for selecting a particular model are:-

  ✓ *Degree of clarity on requirements*—are all requirements known in initiation phase or expected to get clearer with time?

  ✓ *Complexity of the application system to be developed*—simple, medium or complex.

  ✓ Is it product *development from scratch or maintenance* of ongoing product?

  ✓ *Degree of control* the management wants to exhibit in the project or the visibility that is expected from stakeholders in a project.

  ✓ *Expected return on investment* and reporting.

  ✓ *The way product will be implemented* in production or in live environment.

  ✓ *The way sponsors want to spend* on the service provider.

  ✓ The *outcome expected* from the project.

  ✓ Unfamiliar *technology* for developing the product.

  ✓ Funding *limitations of sponsor* due to which they want to have multiple release or iterations rather than spending one time.

  ✓ *Documentation needs*—less or more?

  ✓ *Size of development team* and whether they are colocated or distributed across multiple geographical locations.

  ✓ *Component reusability.*

  ✓ *Cost and schedule limitations.*

  ✓ *Architecture and reliability* of the system.

- Usually agile and waterfall are most widely used models but others like RAD are also prominent.

- Agile is the widely acceptable model nowadays and is also replacing waterfall model wherever it can. The benefit agile brings to the table over waterfall is faster delivery, important functionalities get developed first, return on investment (ROI) realisations from the start of project itself, greater degree of client control, less rework, less documentation, high visibility, and great flexibility in accommodating changes as products are developed iteratively using small functionalities or features called user stories.
- Agile is usually practised with a small team, say one with the size of 6 or 7. If team size is greater, teams can be divided into multiple scrum teams.

Risk #43–Documentation missing for legacy application system or System inventory and documentation provided by client are inadequate

Nothing great was ever built with incomplete information.

–Manoj Yadav

A client might have a legacy application in some technology, say Mainframe-DB2, and they want to migrate this application to new technologies like .NET and Oracle, then they need to provide knowledge and artifacts regarding existing legacy application system to the service provider as base for starting the project.

At times, the documentations provided are not sufficient to understand the complete application system or legacy products, as documentation about certain area is missing or it is inadequate. Often existing business users may not have clarity on few modules of the system.

As developers are not clear on existing application architecture, and its software interface, they will not be able to build the new application system or product with desired functionality. This in turn leads to high rework, increase in schedule and costing, or poor-quality products.

Prevention strategy

- Managers and team to check whether the data or knowledge artifacts about a product are complete. All the aspects of a product like business, technology, databases, interfaces, functionality changes involved need to be covered in detail and evaluated for implementation feasibility.
- Legacy application knowledge transitions can be arranged from subject matter expert (SME) of the client team or service provider. Those who have worked earlier in similar kind of systems and are aware of its functioning can be a good choice.
- The architecture, data, or knowledge given may be insufficient and may not form a complete picture of a product or service. Such incomplete artifacts discovered by a team need to be reported to the client to establish missing links.
- Reverse engineering to be considered where analysis of the application system flow, architecture, and processing to be documented by team. Once finalised, approval of these documentations to be taken from the client and other stakeholders to validate its correctness. This greatly helps in developing the right level of documentation and puts a knowledge support system in place.

Risk #44–Project with strict deadline and fixed budget

Beware the time-driven project with an artificial deadline.

–Anonymous

Service providers may end up bidding for projects which have very strict timeliness and limited funding by the client. Moreover, sometimes the number of resources is fixed by the client as per the nature of the contract. This can be a nightmare for project managers and create a lot of other problems for resources engaged in a project. As a result, organisation simply is not able to profit much from such engagements and ends up losing its reputation in the market.

Prevention strategy

- Sales team to have clear guidelines on the type, domain, and technical needs of the project that the organisation can support and the SPOC senior manager for a particular type of a project. Both sales team and delivery team to work in collaboration during the bidding process. The project which demands huge effort compared to time allocated for completion and less than expected revenue are to be avoided by mutual consensus or renegotiated with the client.
- Processes to be established in such projects based on contract needs and an organisation QMS. Utilise standards, best practices, templates, estimations, and human resources from similar project in an organisation—completed or ongoing, to quicken setup activities before the project starts. This will give an appropriate start to accomplish the goal in quick time. Proper escalation matrix to be defined from the start itself. Lessons learnt to be documented and implemented in the project.
- Greater degree of control is required for such projects. Daily meetings to be conducted for reporting the status and addressing risks/issues in a project. These risks or issues to be resolved on immediate basis without delay by the project manager and the client, to achieve high performance from team, and execute the project within limited schedule. Senior management reviews to be conducted on periodic basis.

- Proper resource allocation to be done based on the skill set of resources and tasks involved. Use critical path method (CPM) to figure out the shortest duration in which the project can be completed without any delay. This includes identifying critical tasks of the project and then executing other activities in parallel with them.
- Resources to be allowed only planned leaves and that too after some months and through proper capacity planning. Project manager to advocate planned leave culture and have backup resources to do the job. Cross-training to be promoted for such projects where another team member can execute the task in absence of a primary resource so as to deliver on time.
- Managers for such projects should be hired keeping past success records in mind during interview process. Highly committed individuals with good performance history to be hired for such fixed budget projects, thereby avoiding any delay in delivering the project due to leadership issue of the project managers. Similar kind of interview process can be put in place for the project team members.

Risk #45–Unrealistic estimates of work by client

Expectations are dangerous when they are both too high and unformed.

–Lionel Shriver

There are certain projects in which the client exhibits greater degree of control on project activities than the vendor management. These projects are also termed as client managed projects.

In such projects, the client may give estimates which are less than required by the team for carrying out the development or maintenance task. However, the actual effort and time that is required by the team for carrying out the task exceeds in reality.

In such a situation beware and don't directly start working on the task or work provided by the client as this may end up eating your project budget based on contract type. Your company would have to bear additional expenses, in case the fund allocated by the sponsor for the project is consumed even before the contract end date is reached.

Prevention strategy

- Client given estimation for the project to be re-evaluated internally by the vendor project team by doing proper impact analysis of the work.
- Come up with an *estimation guideline* that can be used to arrive at the actual estimation figure that you would need to complete work, based on past experience or parametric estimates by analysing number of impacted systems, components, screen, fields, number of files, and deciding their relative complexity.
- *If significant difference in internal and client provided estimates is noticed*, vendor management to discuss with the client and bring forth justification of the actual effort that will be required to complete the project, considering impacted components and effort involved. Most of the times, when justification is genuine, the client will understand and change their estimates to adjust with what you need. They can then extend the schedule and the budget of the project or allow more resources to complete it on time. Use your *negotiations skill* for the same.

Risk #46–Non-availability of SME from client's end

Sometimes it's not the people who change, it's just their priorities that do.
–Curiano

The client SME (Subject Matter Experts) may become

unavailable due to their planned or unplanned personal commitments, emergency or their career priorities may change with time leading to shift to another department or organisation. All these can become a risk for the project, leading to delay and bottlenecks in the project performance, mainly when SME exhibited the kind of knowledge and leadership qualities that others rarely have.

Prevention strategy

- Senior management to request from client management such cooperation from the beginning of the project itself. The client director or manager to inform vendor management about the planned leaves by SME in advance and arrange for the backup when situation arises.
- Document escalation matrix for the service provider in contract itself for such risks. Any mitigation or contingency plan to be prepared earlier itself during initiation.
- Project team to check impact on overall schedule due to non-availability of the client SME and bring it to the notice of senior management.
- If SME unavailable for short duration, check the transition schedule with SME and discuss if it can be adjusted by planning some other activities for team during the days they are unavailable, without affecting the constraints cost and schedule. This will ensure team is occupied and finishing some other part or activities of project so as to remain on schedule.
- Requesting client managers to check if vacation can be postponed until the transition gets over or arrange for backup SME until SME resumes office.

Risk #47–Non-cooperative SME from client's end

Exposing yourself to various cultures is so vital towards personal growth.

–Dau Voire

Sometimes your project team ends up with the client subject matter experts (SME) or client management team member who doesn't value your culture as they consider you or your country to be inferior. It could also be a case that they don't value your time and behave rudely with your project team members.

This not only disrupts the work environment but also triggers various other risks for vendors like loss of reputation, future business, legal hazards, delay in deliveries, etc.

Prevention strategy

- Before the start of project transition, client's HR to conduct sessions for their SMEs related to professional etiquette, code of conduct with vendors, cultural training, and outsourcing topics.
- Vendor management team to discuss with client management or SME the roles and responsibilities involved in the project and work. They need to present clearly the expectations for fulfillment of duties as per the contract and extend all kinds of cooperation for the benefit of the project, prior to working with them.
- Senior management to have meetings with the client management and the SME on regular basis to discuss the progress and for resolving any operational issues during the entire duration of project.
- Project team should have proper escalation matrix defined to deal with any behavioural or contractual issues with the client teams.
- In case of any issue with the client SME, no mails to be directly written to the client management or SME by the team members. On behalf of team members, the senior management needs to talk to the client management through proper escalation mechanism route, and address

the issues with SME when it becomes a bottleneck for the project progress or when violations of any human rights occur.

- Actions such as cultural training, motivational training, or career planning for the trouble causing client SME can be arranged and even eviction can be planned when need arises after multiple warnings.
- Management to check with the client for any backup or alternate SME in case an issue remains unresolved for the benefit of both the parties and in the interest of the project.

Risk #48–Change in client management team

If there's one thing that's certain in business, it's uncertainty.

–Stephen Covey

It may happen that the client enterprise is acquired by another company, or its existing executives resign. Often, they could be asked to handle some other department due to which their roles and responsibilities can undergo a change.

All these situations at client organisation can lead to leadership change for the project. The vendor project team's commitment and focus may suffer, causing an impact on their work and performance. This is mainly due to the lack of vision, guidance, and focus which can extend decision making time by the management, create confusion, increase rework, cost, and affect quality.

Moreover, the project schedule can be severely affected if *work products and deliverables* are not approved by the previous client team member. The new executive can take more time to understand it, can consider it as a risk to his/her job, and delay the things until clarity is achieved.

Prevention strategy

- Vendor management to schedule meeting with the existing client to address issue of such changes in leadership and discuss its impact on the committed project.
- Ask for the plan from the existing client management regarding the future of the project, the effect on the funding plan, impact on schedule due to change in leadership, and take appropriate actions to reduce risk.
- Vendor management to have a town hall meeting with the project team and inform them about the same. They need to clear their doubts. Request them to extend their cooperation to the organisation and remain committed to the project outcome.
- Management and team to ensure all necessary sign-offs are in place from the existing client management so that they are fairly insulated from the changes in a client team.
- Management to do periodic follow-up with the client, reassess this risk, and minimise its impact on the project. They need to facilitate and ensure smooth handover of the project to the new client leadership.
- Project managers and team to schedule meeting with the new client managers and brief them on current status, any roadblocks or risks foreseen by the team and further action plans. This helps to establish the commitments and set clear expectations.

Risk #49–Not handling client's FTEs properly in a project

Roles and Responsibilities must be clear.

–Ian Watt

Professionals who work in agile with onsite-offshore model, in addition to the involvement of the client scrum master and product owner, also often find involvement of *full-time employees (FTE)* of client company in a project.

Clear demarcation of responsibilities becomes necessary between the FTEs and vendor teams in a project at all times. Not regulating roles can create conflicts and competition between the two parties. This will create confusion as to who is going to take up which role and responsibility. Eventually all these can hamper the interest of the service provider, their reputation in market, project team performance, and delivery quality, making it difficult for them to get a project next time.

Prevention strategy

- Senior managers to discuss with the client or the product owner in agile projects on the role of the FTEs in the scrum team—who is accountable for which tasks, their roles, and responsibilities.
- Assess the impact on the project and ensure overlapping of roles between the client FTEs and the vendor team is minimised.
- Assess whether the project is in the interest of both the parties, is as per the vision and mission of the company, the profit margin, and the risks involved. Continue only when benefits far exceed the risks, otherwise cancel the project and get back to next available opportunity.
- Work with the product owner and scrum master in agile to define the capacity and velocity of each party, their performance metrics, and prioritise which user stories will be performed by whom in each sprint.
- Scrum master to channelise the scrum team and FTEs to achieve results for the client and the vendor, and resolve issues as soon as they arise.

Risk #50–System architecture or design not finalised by client

Design can be art. Design can be aesthetics. Design is so simple, that's why it is so complicated.

–Paul Rand

System architecture or design is the most important deliverable where you give technical specifications of doing things as laid down in the scope requirements. This is also the most important document in SDLC development process that lays down the foundations of rest phases and the product itself. So, you need guidance and confirmation from the client on design before proceeding ahead with rest of the phases like development, testing, and deployment.

Any flaw in design or its delayed approval can impact the project outcome in a huge way and can lead to failure of the product when it is launched in the market. This will not only impact the end users but also hamper the reputation of the client and the vendor due to bad publicity and the complaints in social media later.

Prevention strategy

- Design to be documented by the team after careful understanding of the business case, detailed low-level requirement document of product, the input and output of the system, the 'as is' and 'to be' functionalities needed and understanding the technology in which the solution is to be provided.
- Brainstorm with the architects and experts who already have exposure to similar type of products or technology. Attack ideas to uncover faults in the design approach, then consider the best alternative to proceed further. Use technology that is safe, secure, and robust.
- Develop a quick prototype of the design and improve it further with continuous feedback and iterations rather than waiting for completion of the whole design.
- Maintain the traceability of all business requirements into design document. Ensure all detailed requirements have been covered in the design. Once this is done, have

a walkthrough of the design with all stakeholders being impacted and finalise it.

- Once finalised, get it approved from all the stakeholders including sponsor and business users. Any suggestion by them is to be accommodated for further improvements.
- Any major changes in design post approval to be handled through *change management process* after assessment of impact on the system, costing, scope, and schedule.
- Projects that have significant technical risks and uncertainties should go for *proof of concept (POC)* phase in which design prototype can be developed. This helps to examine whether your idea is going to work or not, thereby allowing you to cancel the project with minimal spending when POC fails.

Risk #51–Acceptance or sign-off delay by business teams or client

Acceptance makes an incredible fertile soil for the seeds of change.

–Steve Maraboli

Once the significant intermediate deliverables like business requirement document (BRD), low-level design (LLD), test cases are completed by the project team, these need to be approved by the client for completeness and for giving a go ahead to the project team for the approach.

Not having this in place or not getting approval on time will delay the delivery and affect the schedule. Moreover, no clear communication to the project team to proceed ahead for the next phase can cause high rework later when requirement, design, or testing goes wrong. Even the client can come up with major change to the requirement document at a later date impacting the costing and schedule of the project.

This could also lead to misunderstanding between the parties and legal issues later.

Prevention strategy

- Get customer commitments on sign-off in the SOW contract itself. Maximum number of days after which acceptance not provided can be considered deemed acceptance.
- Escalation mechanism to report the issues to the client management should be in place.
- Web portal for uploading sign-off documents for each work request to be in place for easy reference, tracking, and avoiding multiple follow-up.
- Involve the client in the regular review meeting and discuss acceptance criteria being met or not or follow-up on any pending approval.
- Project team to have regular follow-up with the client for timely approvals.

Risk #52–Volume of work request has increased drastically from the past

The equilibrium between supply and demand is achieved only through a reaction against the upsetting of the equilibrium.

–David Harvey

Some projects are not just pure development but rather maintenance projects involving small enhancement and support. Such projects can have adhoc request activities too which are unplanned and on demand.

Often, issues in the production environment and service requests from customers due to changing business needs can increase. These can cause additional burden on the resources in maintaining clients' applications *business as usual* (BAU) and exceed existing capacity of the resources agreed with the client.

Prevention strategy

- Check if prioritisation of the requests or deliverables can be done to solve this temporary problem.
- If things persist for more than two weeks, discuss with your client for any plans to increase number of resources in project considering the project work scenarios, and work out possible solutions.
- Analyse the past few months' activities and workload in the project to forecast future capacity needs considering availability of your resource.
- Accordingly, number of resources to be increased or decreased as per the discussion with the client or senior management based on the new capacity.
- Certain percentage of buffer resources to be planned and allowed in the project as part of internal strategy by your organisation for handling extra workload in crisis situations.

> **Tip: Consider allowing additional 10% resources than specified in the project contract with the client as part of your organisation strategy. However, this provision to be exercised only based on proper justifications by the project manager.**

Risk #53–Contractual service-level agreement (SLA) with stringent penalties by clients

You need to look at the level of customer service.

–Rob Colasanti

At times, client-imposed level of service is demanding and accompanied by severe penalties which can cause heavy toll on the project profit margin, in case the project team is unable to meet them while executing the project.

Prevention strategy

- Read your contract document very carefully and check whether any penalties are imposed as part of the service level agreement (SLA) section in the contract. Check if SLA metrics are realistic and if team size and capability is adequate to meet the level of service expected—analyse the past trends and volume of tickets that have emerged on monthly basis, the time it took to resolve them, the effort involved, and the number of resources that were involved in the project.
- If you find a huge mismatch when analysing the past trends, work with your client to reduce the penalties associated or keep your SLA metric goal more relaxed. This could help in reducing the impact on profit margin by either lesser penalty in dollars or reduced breach occurrence. In case the current capacity is inadequate, you can request the client to increase billing for few more resources in the project.
- Proper escalation mechanism to be established in the project for resolving issues related to SLAs.
- Monitoring of the SLA metrics to be done on a daily basis to avoid any misstep in reaching goals and timely reporting to the client. Have periodic follow-up on open tickets, their status, and impediments. Issue tracking can be done through tools like ServiceNow and Jira.
- Check whether on-call support team is required to intimate team members when any production issue arises.
- Root cause analysis (RCA) needs to be carried out for the tickets that lead to SLA breaches. Corrective action should be put in place to reduce such breaches. This will greatly avoid margin hit and increase customer satisfaction.
- *Analyse the customer feedback after closing the ticket on a periodic basis*—weekly or monthly, to understand how satisfied they are with your solution. Have action plan where feedback is not positive for future improvement and learnings.

Risk #54–Cash flow fluctuations during project cycle due to sponsors

They were told there were cash flow problems, that the cheques were in the mail. Obviously, they never got it.

–Christine Jackson

Service provider's projects can face funding issues by the client at any point in the project life cycle.

This can happen as client organisation is probably facing some internal challenges—they are hit in business and unable to make profit like earlier, or new CEO/Director is not allowing the funding of your project due to another strategy in mind. It could be a political or legal issue that forces them to stop funding your project, or poorly managed project by your manager and team compels them to take this harsh decision in the interest of their company.

Whatever be the reason, your project is in jeopardy now and it can be restarted later after short or prolonged delay or cancelled by them.

Prevention strategy

You have no option but to accept such risks but here are a few things that you can do as immediate measure:-

- Senior management to arrange a meeting on immediate basis with the client to understand the issues they are facing and their plan going forward.
- Highlight your organisation's effort to make this project a success and that this action by them can have serious effect on the project outcome. Check with the client for any solution which is beneficial for both the parties.

- If requested to continue the project with reduced funding, check the important roles you need in your project team and continue with them. Release the resources that do not have a billing visibility in the future.
- Sometimes the client wants to hold the project and continue with it after few months when funds become available. In this case, you need to give them some other opportunity since these resources might still be required due to the knowledge and experience they have gained over a period of time in the project. It could be difficult to find a replacement in the market and could affect the project outcome.
- If the client is long-time and you share important strategic relations with them, consult your organisation if they can fund this project themselves. This can be done when funding needed is very less and maintaining relationship holds more importance.
- If you have no other option but to close this, deliver by parting away with the requirements that are low in business value. For example—if you have used MoSCoW analysis, Should-have and Could-have requirements can be parted away with due to budget constraints. Request your legal team to work in the abrupt contract termination process, release resources from the project and collect your pending dues if any.

Risk #55–Expressed customer dissatisfaction

Unless you have 100% customer satisfaction, you must improve.

–Horst Schulze

To control the vendor performance, clients often rate their vendors with the help of *customer satisfaction survey form, often referred to as CSAT.*

Usually it is accompanied by a score or rating termed as

CSAT score or CSI (customer satisfaction index). The terminology CSAT or CSI may differ for industries, but it is usually any feedback report given by the clients or customers.

CSI is awarded by the client based on evaluation of different parameters of the project success like technical, domain, and communication skills of resources, application knowledge of the team, ability to work with the client, delivery quality achieved, management effectiveness, ability to accommodate changes, innovation in solutions, and risk handling abilities of the vendor management and team.

Poor CSAT score is an indicator that the client is not happy with the project outcome and the vendor in areas where they have given low rating in CSAT feedback form. This can even lead to cancellation of the project as per the contract.

Prevention strategy

- Vendor team to do the root cause analysis for the low CSAT received. On a high-priority basis put an immediate action plan for CSAT to control the troubled areas of the project after discussion with the client.
- Use ready templates for preparing CSAT corrective action plan for areas in question by the client. Corrective action can be to organise training for the lacking areas in team competency matrix—domain, technical, soft skills, improving effectiveness of existing processes, or introducing one in the project.
- Management to have independent review from the quality team before sharing CSAT action plan with the client.
- The action plan once shared with the client needs to be monitored on periodic basis for its closure by your project team, and status needs to be discussed with the client and the quality team until no such issues are observed in the project.

- Management and team to measure each process for its effectiveness and work on improving the things so that no issues become apparent in the next CSAT.
- Educate your project team on quality aspects of the product or services, quality management system, and day-to-day activities by which they can add value to the project.
- Team to comply with the scheduled internal audits, close gaps on timely basis by implementing corrective actions as suggested by the auditor.

Risk #56–Prolonged delay from client in giving customer feedback

Quality in a service or product is not what you put into it. It is what the customer gets out of it.

–Peter Drucker

Keeping your existing customer happy with your work is one of the top two rules to run a business. The other one is to win new customers. Your team's job is not only to fix the routine problems that are given by the clients but also to satisfy them with quality focused action in everything they do to run their business as this results in improved customer satisfaction.

CSI/CSAT is desired from the client periodically—quarterly or half yearly by vendors, so that vendors can become aware of the issues in the project and remedy problem areas in the project beforehand. This helps in improving client relationship over time. Good feedback from existing customers is often a testimony that can help to win new customers.

It can happen that the client may refrain from giving CSAT, as evaluating vendor is something they don't like and may delay it. It is possible that they may not be able to find time for it, or they lack awareness on CSAT. Often, the clients may intentionally delay it if they are not happy with vendor performance.

Not getting CSI on a periodic basis can be dangerous for the project and ultimately for the company as project manager and team may not know the problem areas to pay attention to and they may continue to deliver the services in same old way with weak or ineffective processes leading to larger number of customer defects, high rework, increased costing, and extended schedule.

Prevention strategy

- Management to follow-up with the client and request for CSAT evaluation on periodic basis. They can meet the client and discuss the parameters of project success and request physical feedback or through online mediums. Visit by the client on the vendor company premises in onsite/offshore locations can be asked for and their suggestions can be noted. This can be used by the team to improve themselves.
- Periodically, video conferencing can also be organised where the vendor project team and the client can discuss the problem, issues, and risks in the project.
- Track the appreciations and issues highlighted by the client on a periodic basis and measure your progress. This allows you to keep track of the customer pulse and take corrective actions on problem areas of the project. A manager, thus, should ensure that the client is happy in all project management areas.
- Your organisation QMS system should also have process documented for what needs to be done when CSAT not received on time.
- Get your project audited by the internal auditors. This can help to uncover problem areas and correct them before it is too late.

Risk #57–Loss of sponsorship at the beginning of the project

Sponsorship can come to you in different ways. You never know who is watching you, so be 'sponsor–ready' at all times.

–Millette Granville

A sponsor who is funding your project may lose interest during the initial stages of the project itself due to some personal or strategic reason, like their organisation may not want to continue due to other priority projects.

This could put your project in jeopardy as it is liable to get cancelled due to lack of funds in early stage itself.

Prevention strategy

- If you are a service provider and the existing sponsor is not ready to provide funds, your senior management must check with the client management for any other sponsor available to fund the project. If there is no support, escalate the issue to the legal team for cancelling the project.
- In case the sponsor is willing to fund again but currently has shortage of funds, postpone the project activities for some time. Utilise your resources in other strategic initiative by your organisation. Resume work when fresh funding is released to the project.
- Use your project business case, prototype, negotiation, and networking skills to win any other sponsor's interest in your project.
- Seek to raise funds from venture capitalist, crowdfunding, angel investors, or get a business partner. You can even consider alternate ways of funding like leverage from banks and non-banking financial companies (NBFCs) when project benefits outweigh the loan investment involved.

Risk #58–Loss of sponsorship in midway or ending phase of the project

It used to be that death and taxes alone were inevitable. Now there's shipping and handling.

–Bert Murray

A sponsor might lose interest midway as they think that the project is no more beneficial to them. This can also be due to other strategic changes by their organisation or their own priorities have changed with time.

Here are few signs that could help you to detect if this could happen in near term:-

- ✓ Inordinate delay on decisions or sign-offs.
- ✓ Client delaying permission to bill.
- ✓ Client delaying payment of bills raised already.
- ✓ Also, sponsor can quit the project just prior to the contract ending phase of the project due to inevitable reasons.

Prevention strategy

- Your management to discuss with the sponsor and their team for deciding strategy—whether to cancel the project or continue with it. Inputs can be taken from the sponsor to know if the funds will be provided for continuing the project or not. In case they are going to be provided—how and when will they be provided. If sponsors are still not willing to continue, go ahead for its cancellation with the help of legal team. Ask your finance department to work with the sponsor to reclaim any pending dues.
- If sponsor decides to continue with reduced funding, release the excess resources and work with minimal resources. In situation like this, the client may demand project to be finished in quick time. Utilise crashing and fast-tracking techniques keeping a tab on the budget allocated and *critical* tasks.

- If necessary, deliver the project with trade-off on quality and processes so as to complete the *minimal viable product (MVP)* with minimal funding available. Advance product features can be developed later as part of new release when the client has sufficient funds for the same.
- Close the project as per instruction from the client and your QMS process guidelines. Document the lessons learnt for organisation improvement.

Risk #59–Change in sponsorship during course of the project

The corporate environment with its downsizing, restructuring, mergers, and acquisitions has actually become even more of a hothouse for psychopaths.

–Kevin Dutton

Your project sponsor may change during the course of the project.

Risk #57 and Risk #58 dealt with issues when there was no sponsor to fund your project after sometime. However, in some cases you may have change of sponsorship, i.e. one sponsor goes and another sponsor takes their place. It is to be noted that sponsorship change is not always something to panic about as there are pros and cons to every change and a new sponsor can bring fresh perspectives. It could be one of the best things to happen for a project, particularly if the previous sponsor was a bit of a challenge.

Project team can easily lose their focus during the transition from one sponsor to another. The handover should be smooth during this transition such that the impact on the project schedule and costing is reduced.

Prevention strategy

- During this transition time, as a manager, work with the client management to understand the issues. Assess the impact of this risk and take appropriate actions to mitigate it. At times, this delay can be big, so it might be better to slow things until decisions can be made about continuing.
- Ensure to take lead in tracking the budget, assigning the right resources to the project and motivating the resources till new sponsor is onboard.
- Your project team and management to conduct an alignment meeting with the new sponsor and their team so as to set project expectations early—clearly communicate the status of the project deliverables and milestones and set future commitments.
- Business case and project documentation to be discussed with the new sponsor to leverage their support for continuing the project.
- Any issues and help needed from the new sponsor should be communicated by the team.

Risk #60–Test data region not made available as per schedule by the client

Delay always breeds danger; and to protract a great design is often to ruin it.

–Miguel De Cervantes

Test or quality assurance (QA) regions are required for testing of the new or modified software product. Non-availability of test region can add to delay of the project due to insufficient or invalid data for testing.

At times, test data is also dependent on other upstream system which may get late in providing you the test files as they themselves have not received them from client.

Lack of proper test data or region may lead to development of products that can fail to execute in different environments; these may even be incompatible with the other products and may have higher number of bugs.

Prevention strategy

- Project manager to ask the dates on which test data or regions will be made available to the project team. Ensure this is drafted in the test plan during the coding phase or before it.
- Your project team to do the regular follow-up with the client or external teams in advance for the testing phase readiness and progress.
- If testing phase has started and some test files and data have not been received, the same needs to be escalated to the client and other stakeholders.
- Analyse if such testing task is in the critical path. If so, the project team then needs to assess the impact on the project schedule and costing, and suggest client to change the schedule.
- Check with the client if any existing regions or environment can be utilised to do some temporary testing using existing data or by creating dummy data before QA region is made available by the client so as to reduce impact on the project schedule.

PERFECTION HAS TO DO WITH THE END PRODUCT, BUT EXCELLENCE HAS TO DO WITH THE PROCESS.

—JERRY MORAN

CHAPTER 06

ON PROCESS ADHERENCE

THERE ARE well recognised standards, methodologies, and best practices for following quality processes in an organisation like ISO 9000, ITIL, CMMI, Six Sigma, defined for IT and related industry projects, for delivering high-quality deliverables every time. These contain the processes and best practices that need to be followed by the organisation. Adhering to these processes is essential for project success; otherwise it can lead to compliance issues.

Enterprises spend a lot of money on quality management, auditing, training on quality, hiring skilled resources, and improvement initiatives to ensure that they are compliant with these standards. For example, there are more than one million companies around the world which are ISO 9001 certified, which is required for survival in the market. These certifications are symbols of trust and promise that the organisation or vendor management is capable of delivering world-class solutions to the customers.

This chapter explores the risks that occur in a project due to non-compliance, not measuring customer satisfaction periodically, lack of awareness of internal quality management system (QMS), not taking initiative by the project team to improve the client processes, and not defining the standards to be followed that often lead to project failure.

Risk #61–Project disrupts compliance

If you think compliance is expensive–try non-compliance.

–Paul McNulty

Compliance means taking steps to comply with the relevant laws, policies, and regulations of the state, industry, organisation or trade. Compliance, often in IT and related industry in operation management is complying with the best practices, standards, and methodologies recommended as a part of CMMI, ISO, and Six Sigma which are part of your QMS.

A project should always be monitored by independent departments for its compliance on:-

- ✓ Right processes in place and
- ✓ Right products are being developed as per the contract

The above two factors determine the overall quality associated with the product or services and whether project objectives are met or not.

Prevention strategy

- Management and project team to ensure that all the processes are planned and monitored in the project as per the organisation mandates as specified in the QMS and the client needs as stated in the contract. Consult your quality department to help you with this.
- Internal audits and facilitations to be conducted on periodic basis to assess projects. Audit team to provide non-conformances (NCs) and opportunity for improvement (OFIs) in process and deliveries as per the predetermined checklist. The checklist needs to cover all the quality aspects

that are required for verification as per your organisation QMS.

- External audits to be scheduled on periodic basis—quarterly, semi-annual, annual basis or as and when business need arises.
- Corrective actions for audit NCs to be planned timely. These actions to be monitored on periodic basis for their effectiveness and closure.

Risk #62–Absence of customer satisfaction measurement process

Aiming for improvement in service delivery is a continual process, even when no one is watching!

–Manoj Yadav

Periodically (quarterly, semi-annually, or annually) vendors need to request customers to provide their satisfaction level of the services provided by them. We have covered customer feedback issues (expressed and implied) in Risk #55—Expressed customer dissatisfaction and Risk #56—Prolonged delay from the client in giving customer feedback.

However, there are some projects in which a client doesn't insist on any customer feedback evaluation.

These projects, therefore, do not have any process for this. Such projects in fact are more prone to failure or missing project objectives as management and team keep on executing things in a project without aiming for improvements in service delivery.

If you ask the CEO or Quality heads of a multinational organisation, such projects are a major reason of their worry but most of them come to know about it only after a project is lost to competitors. The reason for this is most of the CEO/

Quality Head's focus is on the projects with high stakes, on fulfilling demanding clients' needs, or getting new customers. Often, this information gets lost in communication gap due to many levels in organisation's hierarchy.

Prevention strategy

- Management to take initiative and request the client to introduce feedback processes by convincing them why this is important for both the parties and why your organisation feels learning from them and improving is perhaps the best thing that could happen to your company.
- Management to have special focus on building client relationship in such projects through continuous dialogues and take initiative to inform the client about project status, improvement, and solutions.
- Your organisation QMS system to have process documented for what needs to be done when CSAT process is not in a project. Timely internal audits to be scheduled for all such projects.
- Project team to track and analyse the appreciations and issues on regular work in the project. Internal metrics for level of service expected can be defined and monitored.

Risk #63–Lack of awareness of internal QMS process and templates

Ignorance is always afraid of change.

–Jawaharlal Nehru

Good companies, to remain in business, should ensure their company is compliant with international service quality models, standards, and methodologies like CMMI, ISO 9000, and Six Sigma.

Companies do so to develop trust in their customers for the product or service they provide and in their management team.

In order to be compliant, these companies should develop QMS process and templates, partnering with these institutes or from inputs of expert executives who are aware of quality processes and are certified in these standards and methodologies from recognised institutes. This ensures consistency of the processes, practices or work flow followed in the projects and in organisation leading to improvement in the delivery quality.

However, what happens in the real world is that most of the professionals working on the projects are neither aware of the quality processes nor their organisation QMS. Most of the mandated training programs in quality are conducted by an organisation for freshers who are just out of college and thus are relatively immature and inexperienced during training years. So, they are not able to grasp the concepts well. The laterally hired managers or senior programmers from the market have no such mandates to attend quality programs by the top management when they join any organisation. This leads to communication gap between the organisation's intentions and its workforce. As a result, professionals in market or in company lack knowledge on quality and are unaware about it.

Many professionals, in fact, always complain that quality processes or audit work are a waste and that it's the delivery or engineering activity they regularly do that is extremely important. The reality is that both are equally important. With right processes in place comes delivery quality and certification like ISO 9000 which instills faith in customers about your organisation and your abilities to deliver solutions, as they are the ones who pay your monthly cheques.

Prevention strategy

- The process documents should be drafted and made available in the QMS portal by the quality department team. Personnel to inform of such new templates or change in process through broadcast mails or other communication channels within an organisation.
- Organisation to ensure training of fresh or experienced resources is conducted on QMS along with the quality best practices.
- A good manager and his team should be aware about these helping documents, processes, and templates provided to them on the portal of the company. In case they lack knowledge in these processes, they should work with their quality team to implement such standards and best practices in the project.
- Get your projects audited on periodic basis through the internal and external auditing professionals. This ensures that the CEO and the client are aware about the management's commitment in delivering the right product and services. This can be measured in terms of audit score and NCs (non-compliances or non-conformances) which are given by the auditor post audit to the project manager.
- The list with audit score can be made available to the CEO by the quality department team; low score is an indication that some areas are not within control. He/She, then can personally talk to the concerned managers to correct the issues highlighted in the audit.

Risk #64–SLA not finalised in the contract

For better customer satisfaction you need to know, at what level you need to perform.

–Manoj Yadav

Service level agreements (SLA) are the level of service that a client expects from a vendor. These are usually set by a client or can be based on mutual agreement between your organisation and the client. Usually breach of these levels results in monetary penalty to the service providers.

Service level metrics can be set on any aspect of your project. For example, as per the contract, *defect leakage* of 5% implies product delivered to the client should not have customer defect more than 5% of the total defects by the project team. Accordingly, *application availability* of 95% in the agreement means application should be up and running for users and facilitating business for 95% of the business operation days in a week.

At the same time meeting SLA of just 92% instead of 95% as per the agreement may cause penalty of 2% on the revenue the service provider makes for that month.

SLAs are mostly imposed in production support projects wherein to keep existing business application services running business as usual (BAU) is very critical to the client.

> ***Example:*** **If leading Indian IT company X is not able to support a fortune 500 corporation Z's credit card application business services due to a major bug or error in the code, it can result in wrong transactions of millions of dollars and could lead to threat to the existence of Z as its customers may not trust the organisation anymore.**

Prevention strategy

- If SLA is not finalised in the contract, work with the client to set these so that the service performance can be measured. Define SLA associated with service tickets or enhancement activities. Take help of your quality department team in case you are not sure whether this kind of project is SLA applicable or not or there is any confusion regarding the existing SLA set by the client.

- Set *operational level agreements (OLA)* which is nothing but the internal agreements between the vendor department and other application teams. OLA helps to measure internal service efficiency and helps in meeting overall SLA set by the client.
- Also, in case you and the client are not able to define the SLA due to absence of historical data or relatively new project, work with the customer to agree on the 3-4 months' timeline to study the trends of service tickets and come up with SLAs.
- If project team is finding it difficult to set SLA, use capability baseline published by your organisation as base to set SLA.
- Periodically report the status of the SLA to the clients in review meetings. Root cause analysis of any breach observed to be undertaken and corrective action to be worked upon.

Risk #65–Not taking initiative by project team to improve the client set processes

Initiative is doing the right thing without being told.

–Victor Hugo

Some clients in US and other countries may not be aware of the quality processes and methodologies. However, they want to be more profitable by offshoring their business services to the developing countries like India, China, etc. As a result, at times they are incapable of monitoring the vendor or service provider.

In this scenario, it becomes very important for the vendor management and team to pitch-in and help the client in putting right processes and technical know-how of the things in place. However, in reality, the vendor managers sometimes are happy and satisfied with the relaxed way of working of the client. They do only what the client demands. Down the line, in some years, project contract for the vendor is not renewed as the customer has been unhappy with the product quality delivered, the high rework, and the delay in deliveries.

***Example:* A leading MNC project did not have a *design-sign-off* process in place; instead there was *automated sign-off process* of approval from the client end. As no one at the client end was personally reviewing the design for its completeness, it led to many flaws and issues in the system later due to incorrect technical approach and assumptions made. This ultimately led the client to switch to competitor causing around 77 people in this project to go on bench and loss of multi-million dollars in revenue. This was done by the client in the 3rd year from its inception, when they found that the service quality they received from the vendor over these years was sub-standard. Thus, they decided to put an end to the contract.**

Prevention strategy

- Management and team to guide the client with inputs on gaps in existing processes to have stricter process in place. For example, there should be sign-off from the client on solution approach at every significant phase like design, SIT test cases, and UAT.
- Have discussions periodically with the client and understand their areas of concern. Note the risks and issues they are facing and accordingly help them in achieving their goals.
- Get your projects audited by the internal and external auditors and close non-conformances found in the audits on time. Remain compliant with your quality management system.
- Managers to discuss with the team periodically and understand what more can be done to add value to the client. Look to eliminate waste in project processes and activities. Plan for any automation and performance improvement

that can be done in the regular work.

- Look for opportunity with the existing clients by paying close attention to their needs. Identify any other solution or services that the clients would need in future.
- Train your resources in variety of skills including communication and negotiation. This would help them to improve their performance and serve clients more actively.
- Plan for knowledge sharing session with the client in areas they may be lacking or seek transparency. Remember great battles are always won with teamwork.

Risk #66–Not defining the standards to be followed in a project

Without a standard there is no logical basis for making a decision or taking action.

–Joseph M Juran

Standards to be followed in a project need to be defined. Templates and guidelines that need to be used by the resources for different types of projects need to be documented in the organisation QMS. These are required as part of a compliance to the industry standards, and in delivering consistent quality products and services. There are standards for design, coding, testing, and implementation that are required in each project to be followed by the team for better maintainability of the software and their completeness.

Not having these will create unnecessary confusion among the stakeholders. Moreover, your intermediate deliverables or artifacts may lack details leading to poor delivery quality.

Example: **Maintainability and readability of the developed software will be poor in absence of coding standards. This will increase future cost to fix any bugs or addition of new functionalities in the existing software.**

Prevention strategy

- Manager to request the client during initiation of the project to provide standards related to requirement management and engineering processes. Usually the client will be able to provide you the standards and templates that are required in a project. Manager and team can revisit the standards for completeness and suggest improvements if required. Existing layouts can also be used to design the future systems.
- If the clients do not have their own implementation standards, the service provider team needs to study the existing application system and artifacts provided by the client and develop own standards by working together. This needs to be approved by the client. For example, universally accepted standards for languages like JAVA, C, C++ or industry's best practices can be considered.
- Review checklist to be used in the project as these ensure uniformity in engineering processes.
- Your vendor quality management system (QMS) portals can have standards, guidelines, and templates for different kinds of projects.
- Quality team approval to be taken for the standards, review checklists, and templates that will finally be used by the project team.
- Log all the standards related defects. Perform root cause analysis and take corrective action to minimise such defects in future. Monitor them till successful closure.

Risk #67–Lack of SOP and KEDB

Efficiency is doing better what is already being done.

–Peter Drucker

SOP (Standard Operation Procedure) is the most important document or artifact that is required for maintaining an application. It is widely used in supporting a project.

SOPs are nothing but step-by-step procedures of doing things, troubleshooting screens, handling application software, executing programs and jobs so that services or products are delivered consistently every time.

Unavailability of SOPs may lead to confusion and unnecessary delays in restoring some application service in live environment which can stop the business of a company. This in turn can add to frustration of the business users and can even bring a lawsuit for vendors.

> *Example:* **If a leading Indian private sector bank is unable to process payments due to some technical fault, it will cause huge loss to its customers and breach of trust. In turn, it will impact the market share of the bank in negative way. This technical fault could have been easily resolved on time if the team had readied SOP for the same.**

SOPs repository is usually controlled by the client. Though most of the times SOPs are provided by the business users and the clients, they are often documented by the project team. These can later be used by the team for troubleshooting application or services for which they are made.

In addition to SOP, *KEDB (Known Error Database)* is used in maintenance and support projects. A KEDB contains list of all the errors of a particular application system and the workaround provided by the team or users while restoring the system to *business as usual (BAU)*. This is mainly used as a search engine or knowledge base by the team that helps them to quickly resolve the known or already fixed issues.

This greatly increases the efficiency, accuracy, quality, and reduces complexity, effort, time involved for fixing the production issues by the team. At the same time, it also reduces any kind of risk in production environment as solutions are known, time-tested, and have successfully been applied earlier in the business environment.

KEDB greatly reduces the risk of shutdown of application for long, thereby bringing application to BAU in quick time, minimising impact on users, and saving loss of business for clients.

Prevention strategy

- Always ask your client for existing SOPs for maintaining application or restoring services prior to your project start.
- Always evaluate periodically, say bi-weekly or monthly, the needs of new SOPs, improving the SOPs or deleting the unused SOPs. This should be a part of maintenance process. SOPs which are still required for business need to have their expiry date extended. In case they are no longer required, delete them from repository.
- Clients should be updated on monthly basis on the count of the new, updated, and expired SOPs as part of reporting. This also adds to the credibility of the service provider and speaks of their proactiveness and willingness to serve the client.
- Maintain KEDB for application in tools like Microsoft Excel etc. with all the necessary attributes like incident number, description of issues, root cause analysis (RCA) of the issues, workaround applied, and change request number created (if any) for permanently fixing it.
- Also monitor the effectiveness of the KEDB by reporting to the management and the client on the KEDB utilisation ratio.

KEDB utilisation ratio = (number of incidents resolved from KEDB / total number of incidents received by the project team in a given period)

- Application system with higher KEDB of close to 1 in a month can be an indication of a stable system in which the team already knows the solution and is able to fix them each time by referring to the database. On the other hand, lower ratio < 0.2, can be an indication of an unstable system where the errors each time in the application system are new or the team is not using the KEBD database effectively.

WATCH THE PRODUCT LIFE CYCLE;
BUT MORE IMPORTANT, WATCH THE MARKET LIFE CYCLE.

—PHILIP KOTLER

CHAPTER 07 SURVIVING EXTERNAL FACTORS

THIS CHAPTER explores the risks that are external to the project, over which the project team has no or very little control. Some of these risks could be due to the changes in the market demand or supply, recession, political issues like strict visa policy or shutdown of a particular location due to terrorism or natural disaster, while some others could be due to risk posed by no proper background verification in place by an organisation, not able to manage the interested parties/ stakeholders, dependency on other teams for data, and low adoption of your product by the customers or end users.

Risk #68–High attrition due to better prospects by the competitor companies

If people believe they share values with a company, they will stay loyal to the brand.

–Howard Schultz

A good CEO and senior management should always keep a check on the market cycles. There comes a time when the market recruitment is relatively high while at other times it is low, mainly due to the technology industry performing well sometimes and not so well at other times.

Such scenarios occur in the industry due to the external factors like changes in spending behaviour of business and customers with time affecting demand and supply, disruptive innovations, disruptive technology leading to high demand of some particular technology and low of other technology, economic policies, political scenarios, and regulatory needs.

When the demand for resources with niche skills increases, the companies need to offer better remuneration to its resources in accordance with the market. Not doing so will make the employees switch to the competitors, thereby creating problem for your project in terms of lack of experience, knowledge and skills to carry out even the regular tasks. All these lead to high rework, thereby affecting the project costing and the schedule. Thus, the final product developed is of poor quality and will affect customer satisfaction.

Prevention strategy

- Always keep tabs on such scenarios in the market and measure them against your project. Multiple resignations in the project or in an organisation or discussing with the resignee can also give some clue on factors affecting the market.
- Project manager along with the HR and senior management should try to put some action plan in place to improve the situation in the project. Plan to retain the employee if required by increasing their remuneration or giving them onsite or other opportunity they have dreamt of. Appreciate them, recognise their work, eliminate hierarchy, and take steps to make your work place more relaxed.
- You can even try to reduce the impact by hiring the replacement resource from the market or from other projects in your organisation. The new resources to be trained and cross-training to be promoted in a project.

Ensure documentation of all important work is maintained in a project for easy knowledge transition between resources and reducing dependency.

- Change your HR policy if required to give better benefits to employees when your competitor is doing the same. It is rightly said, *trend is your friend,* so copy the competitor and the market if required. Also, take a note of technology, experience of resources, package associated, and pay as per the market.

Risk #69–Threat due to other service provider teams while working together in a project

If you don't have a competitive advantage, don't compete.

–Jack Welch

Usually huge fortune 500 clients never award contract to a single service provider, but simultaneously to the other vendors too. The vendor teams actually work on different business areas and coordinate with each other to service customers.

Clients do this to create a competitive culture, achieve cost advantage, and reduce risk. That is, they all follow the principle, '*if one company is unable to deliver the product quality and price as promised, others will*'.

In such a multi-vendor project, your organisation should be able to deliver value and product quality at par with the competitors. Not only this, the pricing also should be better than others. Otherwise, the client may not renew the contract and may switch to other competitors.

***Example:* A leading investment bank application support service area can be given to a company A, hile development to B, and maintenance to C.**

Prevention strategy

- RFP response to be planned carefully so as to win the project. Never disclose all your secrets to other vendors and client; keep few things secret that can give you a competitive advantage.
- Artifacts and documents of your project to be handled as per the confidentiality guidelines agreed with the client in MSA contract. Other vendors may have their own guidelines.
- Never share your organisation or client information with other vendors. Have dos and don'ts defined for the project and security restrictions on sharing data outside the organisation.
- Train your resources on different cultures and to collaborate well with others.
- Escalation mechanism to be in place for resolving any confidentiality issues with the vendors or client. Draft your MSA contract with the conditions regarding who will own the intellectual property rights during awarding contract itself and responsibilities of each contracted parties.
- Have employee code of conduct drafted for your organisation and signed by them to avoid problems in future.
- Adhere to all quality processes and improve every time. Ensure resources with requisite skills and experience are available to gain competitive edge. Also, a highly focused client-oriented team is a prime necessity.

Risk #70–Mass release of resources from projects

I was asked what I thought about the recession. I thought about it and decided not to take part.

–Sam Walton

Global recession has hit the world many times. Around four post-war recessions are known that affected the world;

these happened in the years 1975, 1982, 1991, and 2009.

The latest recession, often referred to as the *Great Recession*, starting from December 2007 and ending in June 2009, was by far the worst recession that affected many countries and businesses, thereby causing a huge decline in real World GDP per capita.

Companies were not able to generate revenue due to changes in behaviour of both the 'consumers' as well as the 'business' affecting—*B2C (business to consumers) and B2B (business to business)* trade. All these eventually led to heavy layoffs in all companies of the world—large, medium or small.

During a crisis like above, an employee buyout (EBO), takeover or merger can be announced as a part of some strategic move by the CEO and the board members. Many employees of your company may see it as a risk and eventually end up leaving jobs and switching to other companies as employees don't see your company prospects meeting their career needs.

Also, changes in immigration policies of countries, not allowing other countries to do business, huge documentation needs as mandate, high taxes, and strict T&C in some countries, act as a barrier to every company's growth and business prospects. At times, even these can affect the business revenues and lead to mass layoffs.

Multiple factors like above can end up impacting daily work, schedule, costing, and profit margin in a project, whereas at organisation level getting funds for a new opportunity, attrition, and survival are some of the major challenges.

Prevention strategy

- Management to keep tabs on the developments in the external environment affecting projects like recession, international policies, etc.

- Management to analyse and question the client for the changes in the engagement with the vendor company, impact on project funding, resourcing, and other areas of the project to plan strategy going forward.
- During such turbulent times, cross-train your resources and reduce dependency between the team members by documenting the business and technicalities involved in the project. Steps to be taken to identify the critical resources in a project, thereby releasing only the ones causing minimal disruption to the project in case billability reduction decision becomes paramount.
- The vendor company during such tough conditions can work out with the client and reduce the billing rate or allow credits so as to continue relations, even in the challenging times.
- If there is any impact in an organisation, management should have discussion with the team. Discuss openly about the market impact and how your organisation plans to fight it. Motivate the existing resources so as to minimise disturbance in the project environment and continue adding value to the project. Make them understand that these are part and parcel of any business and that things will be back to normal again in quick time.

Risk #71–Project disruptions due to force majeure events

Safety doesn't happen by accident.

–Anonymous

Any terrorism activity, political disturbance, and natural disaster like heavy rainfall can cause your office to be shut for many days. Even commuting can become a challenge due to heavy traffic, bad road conditions, or political turmoil in your office location area.

Moreover, there could be a risk due to strikes, lockouts, etc.

All we can do is to accept these risks and take measures to minimise the impact of these on the project.

Prevention strategy

- Have force majeure clause drafted in the contract itself by defining clearly the definition of force majeure events between the parties.

  The following elements should be addressed in a force majeure clause:-

  ✓ Definition of force majeure events

  ✓ What happens when an event occurs?

  ✓ Who can suspend performance? and

  ✓ What happens if the force majeure event continues for more than a specified period of time?

- Multicity locations for a project can be planned rather than colocating all resources, as this will mean stopping the entire business for those days. At times, when there is chaos in one city, the team can go to nearby locations, like from Mumbai to Pune to support for few days or vice-versa.
- Employees can be allowed to work from home in such crisis situations, access to client development environment through web can be given. Also, adequate security measures to be in place like using one-time password (OTP) keys, virtual keyboards, and other measures while connecting. This greatly helps for single location projects to continue operations.
- Prepare a *business continuity plan (BCP) or disaster recovery plan (DRP)* for protecting the personnel and the assets that are used by your company.
- *Disaster recovery team* with clear roles and responsibilities needs to be set-up. This team needs to work with various stakeholders and project teams for ensuring adequate backup

and preventive measures to deal with crises at all times.

- Adequate backup servers, backup disks, antivirus programs, software system, and other measures need to be in place for technology and data restorations.
- Management to inform the client about the chaos and the expected impact. Any reschedule or changes to be worked with the client; check if your team members can stretch few extra hours to make up for the loss and schedule.

Risk #72–Test data not made available on time by external application teams

Quality is everyone's responsibility.

–W Edwards Deming

Test data files have to be made available by the client or can be given by other application teams who are part of the upstream system. Project team cannot do much in such circumstances as they have no option but to wait, which in turn can impact the project schedule and its budget when right measures are not taken by the management. At the same time, test data should also be sufficient and relevant enough to do valid testing such that all functionality gets tested else this can lead to bugs in the software developed.

Prevention strategy

- Discuss with the external team SPOC or manager for the file. Most of the time they will be able to help you with this.
- Checking upstream system for the frequency of file availability also at times helps in a project.
- Escalate the issue to the client manager if other application teams have failed to provide test data files on time, to reduce any further delay and impact on the project. Also, reassess

the impact on the project variables. Check with the client for the new availability date.

Risk #73–Failing to keep critical interested parties satisfied

> ***All interested parties must be willing to make significant sacrifices.***
>
> ***–John McCain***

Interested parties can come from inside or outside the organisation. These are in fact a person or a group that has a stake in the organisation. Interested parties may be directly affected by the organisation or actively concerned about its performance. Even suppliers, vendors, contractors, and alliances your company depends on for some service, often referred to as third parties, are examples of interested parties.

Critical interested parties that could affect your project are the shareholders, owners of the society or the building in which your office runs—who can anytime ask you to shift your company to another locality as they have been approached by another party with better offer, government, environmental, political and social organisation with whom your business has to interact and work daily as part of a community.

As can be seen from the above, interested parties help and favour you in setting or supporting your business, so ensure you never upset them. They can directly or indirectly pose a threat to customer satisfaction.

Prevention strategy

- Do assess the impact on your business before taking any decision with relation to interested parties. Always keep a chart ready, with the interested parties and third parties identified based on power, influence, and risk they exhibit in running your organisation, keeping in mind areas for which you depend on them like regulatory, political, social, services, etc.

- Know all the regulatory, social, and environmental aspects that are required in running your project or business. Take help of local authority, HR, admin, reputed advisors, lawyers, etc. in setting the right organisation policies. Foster culture of trust and respect at work place. Ensure win-win approach in your dealing with others.
- Comply with go-green initiatives of government or local institutions; ensure using right accessories for lighting and saving electricity, less paper printing, planting more trees, switching off the laptops and computers when not in use. Do comply with these initiatives and other mandates by the government, state, or local authority as violating these can possibly lead to cancellation of licenses of your business or heavy penalty for non-compliance.
- Pay your dues well in time and comply with rules set by them. Communicate regularly with them. Ensure that finance department is established to monitor financial aspects of your company and develop good relationships with bank managers to clear your funds on time.

Risk #74–Not able to manage key stakeholders–delivery teams, enabling functions, and governance directly involved in the project

All stakeholders must participate in the gains and losses of any particular situation.

–Christine Lagarde

Stakeholders are the people who are directly or indirectly affected by decisions, activities, and outcome of a project while delivering services as promised in the contract.

Broadly speaking, stakeholders can be classified as:-

✓ *Internal stakeholders:* These are within the organisation like manager, project team, HR, admin, etc.

✓ *External Stakeholders:* These are the roles outside the organisation like sponsor, customers, business users, suppliers, etc.

However, stakeholder is a wider term comprising of interested parties too. There are key stakeholders who could be from various departments of your organisation and another team external to the organisation that directly affects the project work.

A good coordination and cooperation between them are required in making the project successful.

Non-active participation or insignificant contribution of even a single key stakeholder can lead to downfall of the project. It actually leads to confusion on scope, low employee morale, productivity issues, high rework, and delay in deliveries leading to poor delivery quality. This is mainly due to communication gap and differences in vision of the stakeholders involved.

Prevention strategy

- Identify all the internal and external stakeholders well in advance before starting work on the project. The list of all the stakeholders can be prepared with their contact details and address by getting help from the sponsor and the client or vendor management involved from initiation of the project.
- Have kick-off meeting at the start of the project with all the key stakeholders to seek their commitment till the end of the project.
- Utilise *RACI model* to categorise all the stakeholders into—*responsible, accountable, consulted, and informed (RACI),* based on their role in completing task or deliverables. It is

often referred to as RACI matrix or responsibility assignment matrix (RAM).

- Have periodic reviews to report on the project's progress, achievements, innovation, and risk mitigation. This ensures that stakeholders contribute and remain committed in making a difference to the project.
- Having internal management review on periodic basis for mitigating risks involved in the project execution and challenges unforeseen.
- *Network with your project stakeholders. Life is not about only work; foster a culture of trust and positive atmosphere while working together. Relationship management is in fact the key to all your professional and personal success.*

Risk #75–Lack of resources due to major festival at offshore or long leave plan of resources

An hour of planning can save you 10 hours of doing.

–Dale Carnegie

There are many festivals in some countries. In India, we have major festivals like Diwali, Eid, Holi, Independence Day, Republic Day, Gandhi Jayanti, etc. Yet it remains one of the top offshore countries to invest in due to easy availability of highly skilled resources, low wages, location, and time zone benefits.

These festivals may clash with those of client countries like US during Christmas, Thanksgiving etc. Apart from this, your project team members might have their personal leave plan of more than four or five days which can impact your schedule. So, we need to have a strategy in place to minimise the capacity issues and reduce delay in delivery of services to the client.

Prevention strategy

- Resources should not be granted leave simultaneously as this can affect schedules and deliverables. As soon as you take charge of the project as a manager, arrange a meeting with all the team members, get to know them, and seek their commitment for entire project duration.
- Resources to be asked to intimate leave planning in advance. Also, adequate arrangements to be worked out by them for resource backup thereby ensuring no impact on delivery. Plan for knowledge transfer (KT) session, if the need arises.
- Adjustments for significant festival leaves can be done in milestones schedule itself as a part of the contract, so that client is aware upfront of these holidays.
- Resources can be asked to work from home if required.
- Sufficient buffer resources, say 10% of the total team size mentioned in the contract to be allowed for critical projects to support during urgency.
- Your HR can introduce compensatory working day for such festivals to make up for the loss of work.

Risk #76–No proper background verification of employees, partners, and suppliers

or

Threat due to third-parties

An employer verification system must be implemented to ensure jobs are not given to illegal immigrants.

–Mitt Romney

Background verification (BGV) is of paramount importance and needs to be completed before bringing anyone on board in a project or an enterprise, as criminal intent, data theft, and system hacking are on the rise.

All the resources or partners should be verified for their education credentials, family backgrounds, past employment checks, social media status, and police records before boarding them on company payrolls and this report should be presented to the client on demand.

Social media verification checks have gained prominence these days. Employers can now check your associations on Facebook, LinkedIn, Twitter, etc. The messages and pictures that are posted there and other internet sites that were visited are analysed to form an opinion about the prospective or the current employees and third parties. These can then be used to reject a candidate for the job, fire existing employees or end partnership.

Not doing background checks of a candidates may unnecessarily lead to issues and risks in a project or organisation later, as discussed above. Apart from this, often these are compliance needs of the client, government, or local authorities.

Prevention strategy

- There are various agencies like Social Intelligence Corporation (SIC) that do background checks for an organisation. Your company can partner with them for such services based on the fees they charge on annual basis or case-to-case basis. HR is to initiate BGV of selected candidates in interview before taking them on company payrolls.
- Project to take only those resources whose BGV process is completed and records are available, as not doing so can even violate the security compliance agreed as part of the contract with the client.
- In case of third party:-
  - ✓ Screening and due diligence program can be conducted as it helps in choosing the right firm to work with. Onboarding process to be accompanied by verification of documents and

certifications so as to minimise any risk.

- ✓ A well thought questionnaire can be rolled out to the third parties asking for their responses in relation to the service desired. The responses received can be evaluated and many potential risks can be avoided.

> ***Example:*** **know your customer (KYC) has become a mandatory norm in every industry. Anti-money laundering guidelines (AML) are also adhered by the banks so as to screen suspicious transactions and know about third parties and customers.**

- ✓ Background information and past history of the third parties with relation to services rendered can be analysed from tools like internet, traditional media, social media, references, and testimonials to make informed judgement on working with someone or not.
- ✓ Scheduling third-party audits across operational, information security, and compliance risk, etc.

Risk #77–Unavailability of onsite resources due to strict visa policy or strict immigration laws

If we want to remain a free and open society, then we have to control our borders.

–Donald J Trump

Visa policies keep on changing—sometimes it is easy to obtain visa for employees and sometimes it's difficult. Changes in political scenario of countries, changes in government policies on international laws of doing trade, and amendments in immigration laws from time to time lead to these developments.

With President Trump led government coming to power and introducing strict measures for the people travelling to US for jobs or obtaining work permit, IT companies from

Asia are under a lot of pressure as they largely depend upon the offshore-onshore structure for making profits with less resources onshore.

The government proposed changes in immigration policy include doubling the per hour bill rates for onshore employees, which can double their monthly compensation salary. This indirectly could create huge pressure on firms in India and the world, as it can hit the profit margins of these companies.

Not much can be done for the above except appealing to the US government through NASSCOM or other trade association and it was done. One has no option but to accept this risk. However, here are few preventive measures.

Prevention strategy

- Your organisation's overseas travel team to track changes in visa policy on a regular basis. Accordingly, employ strategies on the number of visa positions that need to be applied for in a year based on the forecast of the onsite positions in near term.
- Have permanent buffer resource pool at onsite and offshore in your company with visas ready so that immediate vacant positions can be filled on demand.
- Managers to scout for resources with required project skills at onsite or offshore to fill onsite positions in a project. Look to hire by partnering with external recruitment agency if the need arises.
- Consult with HR and look for onsite resources with requisite skills nearing end of their engagements with the projects. Allocate them in advance to upcoming positions in your projects after discussions with them for their willingness, skill fit, and experience required in the project.
- Hire resources with visas on contract from the manpower consultant firms. Contracted professionals will help you

reduce cost as they can be deployed on demand for short term positions as the permanent employees can prove costly in the long term.

- Arrange for training of new resources selected for onsite positions if minor gaps in skill set.

Risk #78–Technology disruptions in a VUCA world

In the midst of chaos, there is also an opportunity.

–Sun-Tzu

Modern day applications like Amazon, Facebook, Twitter, etc. generate and store lot of data per day. To store or make sense from this data, traditional database management system like DB2 cannot be used as the data is huge in volume, is relatively unstructured, and is not fault-tolerant as more machines cannot be added to the existing computer clusters. All these drawbacks with traditional system make Big data technologies much better option for today's organisation systems. This is why most of the customers/users have started preferring applications using it, thinking about the future or current scenario. Also, when it comes to preferring choice of application technology, Java and .NET have become a better option than legacy Mainframes.

A cloud-based infrastructure is today a trend due to faster execution, scalability, capacity, and most importantly low cost. Similar was the case with internet which revolutionised the way business is done. These are examples of *disruptive innovations.*

Big data, Salesforce, Mobile internet, Internet of things (IoT), Automation of knowledge work are examples of *disruptive technology* as these have capacity to alter our lifestyle, the way we work and do business and the global economy itself.

The above two terms 'disruptive innovations' and 'disruptive technology' were used for the first time by renowned author and Harvard Business School professor, Clayton M Christensen.

Prevention strategy

- The vendor can initiate and discuss with the client the challenges that the existing product is facing due to disruptive technology or disruptive innovation. If the client approves the budget, work on solution that can work for their business again. However, this is not easy. The vendor needs to have high skilled resources who are well-versed with the latest technology to take on these kinds of challenges.
- A service company can increase its capability in certain technology by creating a new department with focus on hiring candidates with new age skills like Big data and Salesforce, Cloud services, Mobile technologies, and Digital technologies. Candidates who have prior experience in these technologies can be given preference while hiring. Certifications in such technology also speaks volumes about the credentials of a person.
- Often for a service provider, disruptions are good, as these are times to change strategy of the organisation. For example—clients are eager to spend more on migrations projects during such changing times.
- Promote a culture of continuous learning and development, upskilling, and cross-skilling in your organisation.
- Focus on innovations. Spending about 5% of the revenue on research every year can greatly help in survival during such tough times.

All steps discussed above can be used to gain more projects and trust of the customers in your organisation even in disruptive times. Therefore, Clayton rightly said—*'Disruptive technology should be framed as a marketing challenge, not a technological one'.*

Risk #79–Low adoption of product/service by target end users

It turns out that is exactly what product strategy is all about–figuring out the right product is the innovator's job not the customer's job.

–Ben Horowitz

Often, existing product or service does not go down well with the user and they suddenly or slowly stop using the product developed by you or to undertake service from you.

To explain this better, consider a retail store website as a product. Customer may discard your product for following reasons:-

- ✓ The interface of the website is not good; the background colour, text, and fonts are painful to user eyes.
- ✓ The navigation to different pages and button is quite slow which is frustrating them.
- ✓ Images of utensils, clothes, or books are of poor quality which is failing to generate interest in users.
- ✓ For buyers, only credit card payment is allowed while others like cash on delivery, internet payment, and debit card are not supported.
- ✓ The website is difficult to use and online documentation is lacking details.
- ✓ The website gives a pop-up message frequently which irritates the user.

This is mainly because the customer did not get the kind of *usability or user experience* they were expecting from the website.

User experience is a wider concept than usability. Usability refers to whether the product can be easily used by the users while user experience is what user feels when using a website or a game. It does not take only usability into account, but the need, look, feel, and brand value experienced by the customers.

Thus, your product should have better response time, better aesthetics, should be reliable, should give accurate results every time, be high on capacity, should be easy to train the user through online documentation or any other medium. There should also be a choice for the users to switch to local language mode so that language does not become a barrier and your product gets accepted by users all over the world.

Not ensuring all these will make the user or customer switch to the alternate product. So, plan for usability and user experience before it's too late.

Prevention strategy

- Brainstorm with customers to have a clear understanding of the requirements of the end product. Develop specification and design in incremental fashion with them.
- Design so as to ensure the average training time for user to get ready to use your product is as less as possible (~0 sec).
- Aesthetics, accuracy, performance etc. discussed earlier should be taken care in design and requirements stage itself.
- Study the already existing, widely used competitive products and then develop your product, so that you know what all features you need to provide, as well as what you can do to gain competitive edge.
- Remember to ensure the core of your product; for example—the homepage of a website is simple, and users are able to grasp its functioning by just having a quick glance at it.
- Ensure to make your software interactive or responsive to users. Notification and acknowledgement popup messages to be shown on screen or emailed. These greatly help in enhancing user experience.

> ***Examples:***
>
> *a) 'You have crossed 1,00,000 views today' is a notification.*
>
> *b) 'We successfully received payment of $ 1000' is an acknowledgment.*

Such messages need to be displayed during recovery from errors, exceptions, troubleshooting, backup, and restoration of software. But here's the catch—unnecessary popup messages to be avoided at all cost.

- Independent expert team can be used to check on user experience with end users in mind and their psychology in UAT environment. Suggestions given by them need to be accommodated before launching product.
- Test your application response with small set of target customers prior to launching any product. Their feedback helps to understand possible risks that could come up before you actually launch your product.

GET THE RIGHT PEOPLE.
THEN NO MATTER WHAT ELSE
YOU MAY DO WRONG AFTER THAT;
THE PEOPLE WILL SAVE YOU.
THAT'S WHAT MANAGEMENT IS
ALL ABOUT.

—TOM DEMARCO

CHAPTER

08 PROJECT TEAM CHALLENGES

A TYPICAL project team comprises of a project manager, developers, testers, business analysts or subject matter experts. This chapter explores the risks/challenges for which they are directly responsible like not prioritising activities, inadequacy in estimates, not selecting the team with right skills, inadequate testing, inefficient knowledge management practices, and not doing root cause analysis properly.

Risk #80–Not properly tracking the project tasks and deliverables

It is not enough to be busy…the question is: what are we busy about?
–Henry David Thoreau

Tasks are assigned to the project team by the client or internal management. Apart from the scope-based activities in the project, there are other activities in the project like quality activities, defect prevention activities or performance improvement activities. For the managers, these include working on the proposals, monitoring resources, reporting to higher management for reviews or working with various other stakeholders in an organisation.

A project manager needs to be very careful that the resources are involved in the right project activities at the right time. This ensures that the milestones mentioned in the contract are met.

Project team and management can anytime lose track of activities and end up blowing the schedule and budget allocated if right controls are not established in the project to monitor activities.

Often young professionals don't prioritise their activities for the day. They need right guidance by the management and leaders to help them with prioritisation of their activities.

Prevention strategy

- Carefully select intelligent software tools like Rally for agile or MS Excel to keep track of tasks, status, effort involved, and ownerships of tasks. Usually every work allocated by the client can be divided into major and minor milestones. The tasks belonging to these can be listed to enable the resources to have a clear picture of project activities.
- Project managers or leaders to delegate task to the resources based on their skills, experience, and availability. Keep tabs on the activities your team is working on, at any given time.
- Have periodic review meetings with the team members and discuss work status. Understand dependency between the task and resources to prioritise things well in the project. This also helps in resolving the impediments in achieving milestones.
- Always figure out the critical tasks for completing a project and accordingly lead it to completion by giving them more focus and finishing without delay in shortest time. This can be figured out by using critical path analysis.
- Keep schedule in mind. Track task progress against the schedule. Utilise techniques like fast tracking and crashing to complete the project on time.
- Measure the effectiveness of the task completed by analysing

metrics like rework %, phase containment effectiveness (PCE), effort variance, schedule variance, and schedule slippage.

- Ensure that the task progress is discussed in periodic review calls with the client to keep them informed about any issues or risk. Any reprioritisation request by them to be taken into account.

Risk #81–Too optimistic or pessimistic estimates by project team

Good estimate = cost saving + relationship + peace of mind - chaos - rework.

–Manoj Yadav

Giving right estimates is the most important thing required from a project. This ultimately is responsible for arriving at the cost of completing the project. Thus, the profit margin to a large extent depends on how well the estimates are given by the service provider, as costing or pricing is the most important factor for delivering value to the client.

Too high estimates can lead to costing issue with the client and not winning the bid for the project, while too low estimates can lead to hit of the profit margin of the service provider. So, a balance is required in giving the right estimates.

There are various techniques of estimations that can be used to arrive at the estimate of the project. The most common ones are expert judgement, parametric estimate, analogous estimate, and three-point estimate also known as program evaluation and review technique (PERT).

- ✓ *Expert judgement* is using SME or expert advice to give estimate.
- ✓ *Analogous estimate* is using similar past projects to estimate

cost or duration of a project.

✓ *Parametric estimate* is using different parameters or variables of a project to arrive at estimate; essentially it involves using number of impacted units and their complexity to arrive at the estimate.

✓ *Three-point estimate or* PERT estimate is used to average out the optimistic (O) and pessimistic (P) estimate given by formula (O+4M+P)/6 where M is most likely estimate.

For agile projects, a team can arrive at the estimates using agile techniques like planning poker, affinity grouping, and others.

Prevention strategy

- Utilise estimation guidelines relevant to your project to arrive at better estimates. These can be prepared based on the nature of work in a project, different types of tasks in a project and their complexity. Once approved by the management or client, the same can be used by the team to arrive at the right estimates.
- Do thorough impact analysis as per the problem statement and identify the impacted components—programs, files, systems, databases, and stored procedures. Prepare estimation sheet in agreement with the estimation guidelines. Utilise one of the techniques discussed above for estimates or combination of these.
- Where estimates are high, they need to be worked out with the client and corrective actions are to be taken to update it until both the parties are in agreement. Redefine estimation if necessary.
- Automate some processes, make use of reusable components to add to further reduction in estimates, hire skilled resources, and procure some optimising tool that can reduce your effort in completing some task.

Risk #82–Not creating WBS and identifying the critical path

Running a project without a WBS is like going to a strange land without a roadmap.

–Anonymous

A large work needs to be divided into a set of activities or tasks. These tasks when properly ordered and executed sequentially or in parallel, ensure that the project is completed in minimum time. This can be done with the help of *work breakdown structure* (WBS) planning in which all the tasks required to complete a project are identified, their dependency analysis is done followed by prioritisation of tasks. This organises team work into manageable sections.

WBS is the basis for identifying the 'critical path' that can give the minimum number of days required to finish a project by identifying its critical tasks and effort involved in them. Then the manager can utilise resources effectively and ensure they get completed without delay. Not doing this will lead to spending a lot of time to finish the project. Moreover, project teams will be lost in doing low priority activities that may not lead them towards their destinations. Therefore, it is rightly said, *'A project without a critical path is like a ship without a rudder'*.

Not effectively utilising the resources on tasks will reduce your performance, impact schedules, increase cost, eat up your organisation's profit margins, and leave the project objective unmet. Having WBS and better task management not only gives maximum optimisation on schedule but also protects your project team from burnout on weekends and nights.

Prevention strategy

- Ensure you create WBS of your projects early by understanding the scope of work in the contract.
- Prioritise the tasks, sequence them, set these interrelated activities as groups. Also, check activities that can be completed in parallel.
- Allocate the days of work that will be taken for each activity considering the number of resources assigned, their availability, and effort per day of each resource.
- Identify your critical path using critical path method (CPM). The minimum days thus determined to complete the project should be your project schedule that needs to be adhered to. Any deviation from this goal can lead to more cost.
- Execute the activities by ensuring focus on critical tasks and other activities in parallel with them.

Note: You can read about CPM techniques for arriving at the project schedule from PMBOK as detailing them is not in the scope of this book.

Risk #83–Not establishing traceability

Without planning for traceability in a project is like going on a safari and then never coming back.

–Manoj Yadav

Traceability is to establish the relationship between different phases of a methodology selected for creating a product or delivering any service. This can be established by means of document called requirement traceability matrix (RTM).

Example: **In waterfall model of software development, traceability is established between requirements, design, code components, and test case created for validating each component.**

It is often bi-directional in nature, which implies that from requirement document we should be able to track the design, code, and test case elements created for the project; or from test cases document we should be able to arrive at the components and the business description in the scope document.

RTM is the best practice and is used mainly in large or medium-sized development or maintenance projects as it avoids rework when any change request is raised by the client asking for some modifications again. This ensures completeness in deliverables.

Not creating RTM would lead to high wastage of time and effort in analysing again which requirements, design, code components, and test cases are to be modified as a part of new changes recommended by the client, creating confusion for the resources. All these can lead to high rework, high cost, and poor delivery quality as some functionality is bound to be missed by the team.

In Agile, these are established with the help of tools like Rally. These keep track of the user stories, its tasks, acceptance criteria, test cases, etc.

Prevention strategy

- Establish usage of the RTM templates from the beginning of the project itself.
- Use ready templates for requirement, design, and writing test cases. Relate section numbers in the design document with corresponding business functionality number in the requirements document. Associate test case of a component modified with its design and its requirement such that it becomes bi-directional in nature.
- Use it to analyse affected components whenever there are any changes in the requirements or design.

- Maintain it during the entire duration of the project.

Risk #84–Not knowing the policies of own company and other departments

Ignorance is a voluntary misfortune.

–Nicholas Ling

A successful project manager needs to know his/her own company's policies, department processes, and guidelines that would directly help to work with other departments like HR, Admin, etc. This knowledge comes in handy when it comes to leave planning, extra compensation for stretching beyond regular hours of working, appraisals, awards and reward recognition, or managing overseas program for the resources.

This is required to manage the most important asset of a company—*the employees*. This helps to motivate them and to maintain goodwill of the company. Otherwise, the resources' productivity or your planning of the project operation will not be effective.

Prevention strategy

- Project managers and team need to go through the company policies and guidelines to understand organisation culture and to work effectively with the other departments.
- Connect well with your team members to understand the problems they could be facing and improvements they seek from your organisation, and support them with the solutions.
- Keep record of the accomplishments of your team members to measure their performance, give feedback, and award or reward them for their achievements.
- Check on the release policies of the resources from project. Mostly companies have limitation of few years for resources

after which they can change the project in which they got assigned by the HR for seeking career changes or limitation of few months as notice period. You need to know them, as these could impact your project when multiple resources ask for release or resign and you may not have backup resources to perform the job in hand, leading to knowledge management issues in the project.

- Besides, there are polices on anti-corruption, gift policy, anti-harassment, and things that could cause conflict of interest with the organisation. Being aware about them helps to protect your rights and prevents you from getting messed up in a wrong deal.

Risk #85–Inadequate or incorrect test cases by team

Quality is never an accident. It is always the result of intelligent effort.

–John Ruskin

How well your project team has understood the requirements? How good is the design and how effective is the coding? All these can be realised only in the testing phase. So, the testing phase is a very significant phase as you test your product in reality here and tangible benefits of product can be realised in this phase only.

Comprehensive test cases need to be written covering all the aspects of the new functionality changes requested by the customers, else it could lead to bug in the code or few functionalities getting missed. These are created prior to implementation phase.

Various test conditions and expected behaviour needs to be captured by the testers. This should be followed by extensive testing and recording the actual results before delivering final product to customers.

Preventive strategy

- Understand your requirements well. Know your system input-output flow well and the impact on it due to the changes requested by the customers.
- Use boundary value analysis (BVA) or equivalence class partitioning (ECP) to cover your test data aspects in creating right test cases.
- Ensure test case is written as:-
  - ✓ *Simple and readable*—plain and simple English language to be used for writing conditions.
  - ✓ *Accurate*—to the point with accuracy in input data conditions and output results.
  - ✓ *Crisp*—short sentences with no unnecessary steps or words and yet covering the complete unit condition to be tested._
  - ✓ *Good Coverage*—all functional and non-functional aspects of application to be covered along with positive and negative test conditions.
  - ✓ *Supported with data*—input test data provided to program and output data or behaviour expected to be listed.
  - ✓ *Traceable*—capable of being traced to requirements.
  - ✓ *Repeatable*—can be used to perform test over and over again.
  - ✓ *Reusable*—can be re-used when necessary.
- Get your test cases reviewed by peer, then by the client. Check for completeness of test cases by ensuring that a test case is there for a functionality given in the requirement or specification document. Maintain traceability.
- One of the things that you can do is start writing test cases early in the requirement or design phase to achieve better clarity on it.

Risk #86–Inadequate testing by team

Be a yardstick of quality. Some people aren't used to an environment where excellence is expected.

–Steve Jobs

There are various types of testing—functional and non-functional testing.

For functional testing of a system, there are primarily four testing levels in software engineering. These are— unit testing, integration testing, system testing, and acceptance testing. Some of these are performed at unit or component level while others are incorporated considering the group of components or entire system.

Besides, there is non-functional testing in areas like performance, reliability, security, etc. There are others also like black box, white box, alpha testing, beta testing, which are recommended for product companies.

Every kind of testing has a specific purpose, so look carefully in the contract or test strategy for what is specified. *Don't skip any specified testing recommended by the users as this can affect services or product later when it's delivered to the client or made 'live' to the users.* At the same time, all kinds of testing may not be applicable for your project or your purpose, so ensure you plan out the relevant types of testing that will be required for your project.

Test strategy and test plan are two most important documents used during planning this phase. Test plan is usually narrow in scope than test strategy and is more detailed. It is created by your testing manager rather than a project manager and has details like testing types, specific testing to be performed, the acceptance criteria, when it will be done, how will it be done, who will provide test data, who will execute, and finally who will provide sign-off on test results until implementing code to 'live' production environment.

Prevention strategy

- Choose the testing applicable to your project scope by understanding the factors like nature of the product, size, amount of data that your product is going to deal with, number of systems or database affected by it, where/how your software is going to run, interfacing applications, number of users it will interact with at a given point of time, scalability, portability, etc. Ensure all testing recommended is performed without skipping any.
- Draft test cases covering both positive and negative test cases. Check completeness and validity of test cases; get it reviewed by seniors or from client.
- Monitor the execution of each test case and its results. Failed results to be logged as defects and fixed.
- Run multiple test cycles to validate the correctness and completeness of testing.

Risk #87–Inadequate test data for testing

All code is guilty until proven innocent.

–Anonymous

It cannot be verified without test data if the given product is working or not and has all functionalities that were requested in the requirements. Test data is very important for testers as well as programmers as both rely heavily on them for their testing activities.

Right selection of test data is paramount for project's success without which quality of various types of testing cannot be ascertained. This can allow test cases to pass with bug in a software product causing problem for the users.

Test data can be generated by using software tools or can

be produced manually. Some parts of the data may be used in confirmatory way to test a given software functionality while others can be created to challenge it.

Carefully prepared test data is even more important for testers as they are looked down upon by the programmers for the defect logged by them when testing is executed with an improper test data. This at times questions their credibility.

Prevention strategy

- Time and cost to produce test data along with its quality to be taken into account for successful project execution.
- Don't postpone test data preparation till testing phase. In fact, it needs to be created in advance much earlier than testing begins.
- Ensure test data created or provided is adequate and sufficient for carrying out testing. Do some dummy testing with a sample of data to validate the test data for correctness and fulfilling the testing needs before proceeding for full-fledged testing.

> ***Example:*** **If your program needs to be tested for all customer records after year 2005 located in India, having a file with test data prior to 2004 and related to US does not make sense. Therefore, it becomes invalid test data.**

- Make use of different test data and test regions for carrying out different types of software testing. Test data to be prepared for every written test case.
- Regularly update your test environment for test data perhaps by production live data. Any kind of old data is unreliable for carrying out testing activities.

Risk #88–Inadequate work products and deliverables review

Review your work. You will find, if you are honest, that 90% of trouble is traceable to loafing.

–Ford Frick

A large number of projects fail due to inadequate review. These can be due to the factors mentioned below:-

- ✓ Self and peer review by appropriate stakeholder not in place.
- ✓ Reviewer approves them by just having superficial look without going into details of the work done by the reviewee.
- ✓ Lack of review causes severe defects in analysis, design, and implementation phase. This causes defects to multiply at each stage, affecting product quality which ultimately affects relationship with your customers and your credibility in the market to deliver quality solutions.

Prevention strategy

- Ensure sufficient amount of effort is spent on reviews in each phase. Make it a habit in your project to spend at least 10% effort on review. According to Roger S Pressman, the expected cost to fix defects increases during the product's lifecycle.
- Ensure review is done by somebody more experienced than reviewee or of equivalent level before delivering to the client.
- Utilise review checklist after each phase like analysis, design, coding, testing, etc. This ensures all aspects and details of intermediate deliverables are taken care of. Log all internal review defects in defect logging tool, identify root cause, and take corrective actions to reduce them.
- Measure the effectiveness of the review process by measuring metrics like review effectiveness, code review effectiveness, review rate, test rate, and improve your team efficiency by having corrective actions for the inefficient process.

- Management to ensure control over communication through emails, etc. that goes to the client or stakeholders. This helps in avoiding confusion between the stakeholders and in maintaining good relationship with the client.

Risk #89–Security threats due to non-masking of sensitive data

Confidentiality is the essence of being trusted.

–Billy Graham

Project artifacts can have client sensitive data. For example, often sample records from live system are used to create the test data files for manual or automation testing. These details are shared with the stakeholders during test planning or verification which can then easily leak to the parties who are not supposed to view the content, knowingly or unknowingly. This kind of practise is to be avoided as it leads to security compliance issues with the customers.

Prevention strategy

- Have customer agreed security guidelines in place for conducting a project. Have acceptance from the resources before boarding them on the project.
- Test data file to be always masked for sensitive data of customers like SSN, customer id, customer address, bank details, assets owned by them, their healthcare or financial details, and other important data that the client may not want to share about their customers. Often, they have binding agreements with the third parties to keep the data confidential.

> ***Example:*** **Health insurance portability and accountability act (HIPPA) in Healthcare industry bans sharing personal information of customers for health care providers in electronic format.**

- Automation of masking data process can be done where the project team can run automated software tools and jobs that will randomise the test data once run.
- Having test data ready environment provided by the client with dummy or tweaked data.
- Any data leak incident to be taken seriously and preventive measures to be communicated to the team. Appropriate penalty and punishment for not following the guidelines need to be in place.
- Records of various artifacts to be kept in the client environment and not in your system machines. Any softcopy or physical papers with client sensitive data to be destroyed by the team.

Risk #90–Inability of a scrum team to attend ceremonies of agile

Adaptation is a profound process. Means you figure out how to thrive in the world.

–John Laroche

Agile methodology emphasises on participation by all the team members called *scrum teams* to be present in all the ceremonies like daily scrum calls, sprint planning meeting, sprint demo, retrospective calls along with the scrum master (SM) and product owners (PO). Practising such methodology becomes difficult in onshore-offshore model where there is a huge time difference between the client's locations and offshore location._

For example, USA has seven different time zones. The time difference between the USA CST (Central Standard Time) and Indian IST (Indian Standard Time) is of 11.30 hours which makes it difficult for the Indian and other Asian offshore resources to participate with the team located at US.

Due to this sponsor or vendor may decide to skip the contract. This means loss to the vendor as they lose business.

Prevention strategy

- Tailor-based approach can be adopted for agile ceremonies in consultation with the client.
- Vendor resource at onsite can act as a mediator between the offshore based scrum team and SM. Thus, they can help in story understanding, status updates, and give demo on behalf of offshore based scrum team.
- Offshore team to report to onsite for ceremonies' updates—daily scrum, sprint planning, demo, etc.
- Offshore resource of vendor can also opt to work in shifts rather than losing the valuable contract.

Risk #91–Not keeping track of the skill gained by resources over the duration of the project

Great things in business are never done by one person. They're done by a team of people.

–Steve Jobs

Hiring the resources as per their skills and proficiency is of utmost importance in selecting the right team for your project. The candidates need to be hired in accordance with the job description of the position or role. You need resources with good technical, domain, soft skills, experience in relevant technologies used in a project, and above all the right attitude. This is often referred to as competency mapping.

At the same time, your team member may not be good in all the skills required in a project. For example—some may be expert in technical skills like Java but lack application knowledge, others may have good domain knowledge but lack technical skills.

Also, some resources may leave the organisation or project and others may replace them causing lack of knowledge in the team. Moreover, the upcoming positions might demand new skills when your project grows. It is therefore important for the manager to track the skills and aptitude of resources to manage the talent pool for the project at all times.

Prevention strategy

- Always ensure candidates are selected after matching skill set needs mentioned in the 'job description' for a given 'job role'. Talk to the candidates and understand the expectation of the person you are hiring for your team. Hiring can be done from external markets or from other projects in the organisation itself.
- Assessment of candidates can be done based on interviews, discussions, evaluation against the test questionnaire or through their professional certifications. Also, prior accolades, academics, and extracurricular activities speak volumes about the candidate and their personality, so use then to your advantage while hiring. This will ensure desirous and meritorious candidates with right skill sets are selected for the project.
- You may not get all the skill set required as per ideal expectation of the job role, so, you should be prepared for it. Instead set up a team that has the right balance of all the skills and experience required in the project.

> ***Example:* Ramesh has current proficiency in Java language of 2, while 4 is expected for job role. This indicates training is a necessity for him to perform well in the project.**

- Track the expected level of skills to perform the job effectively in the project against the current proficiency level of the team member. Promote training to reach the expected level.

- Maintain skill tracker in a project. Periodically evaluate the skills of your resources, promote cross-training, cross-skilling, and on-the-job training (OJT) to meet competency needs of a project.

Risk #92–Not carrying out the root cause analysis of the defects on periodic basis

We cannot solve our problems with the same thinking we used when we created them.

–Albert Einstein

Root cause analysis (RCA) of defects to be done on periodic basis. The basic purpose of doing RCA is to find the 'harmful factor' or 'the source' of defects or issues. It is a useful process for understanding and solving a problem permanently rather than just a workaround. RCA helps to identify the primary cause of why something is not working which could be responsible for multiple secondary issues.

Often, defects logged are used to analyse the issues in the project. This is done by first identifying the root causes of the defects in the project and then applying the 80/20 rule on the identified causes.

By implementing corrective actions for major factors affecting the projects we can address the gap in project processes like lack of knowledge, lack of standards, requirement, design, and testing issues etc. as these things lead to high rework, high cost, delayed milestones, and poor-quality deliverables.

Apart from the above issues, analysing the defect(s) uncovers faults in the application systems and bugs in the software products. All these gaps when not addressed at the right time may lead to unstable application system with lots of issues for users, causing system to remain down most of the times and make it unreliable. Eventually it could lead to ending of the contract by the client as value expected by the client is not delivered.

Prevention strategy

- All internal and external defects leaked to customer to be tracked to closure immediately by the team for delivering quality products or services to the client.
- Purchase or develop in-house defect management tools that can be used to log all the defects and analyse them.
- Ensure each defect that leaks to the customers is regarded as severe issue and RCA including resolution is provided to the client on immediate basis to give seamless service experience to them.
- Implement corrective actions and monitor till successful closure.

Risk #93–Lack of knowledge management and KT transitions

Knowledge management is a bit like travel insurance–you only wish you had it when it is too late.

–O'Neil, A

Knowledge transitions (KT) are required so that the resources can effectively understand the application system in hand, its input and output files, its interaction with other application systems, the processing and reporting it does for business, and the existing architecture.

Without KT, engineers will not be able to understand the specifications. Thus, they will be unable to design or construct the systems.

KT are a part of Knowledge management process which is nothing but creating, sharing, using, and managing the information and knowledge of an organisation or a project.

Knowledge management is equally important for the senior management to understand the customer expectations and align the corporate strategy with changing needs of the business.

Knowledge management is linked to better and faster decision making, increased rate of innovation, and better communication. It greatly increases the efficiency and productivity of the organisation as ideas, perspectives, experience, and information are shared which greatly helps in making an informed decision.

Not utilising the best practices and lessons learnt from the past projects will result in poor planning for future projects thereby reducing profit margin due to increased schedule, indecisiveness, and high rework.

So, this process is of utmost importance in running the projects.

Prevention strategy

- KT transitions need to be organised during the initiation of the project itself. These transitions can be done by the subject matter experts (SME) or business users who are well aware of the system.
- Maintain repository for knowledge documents on domain, technical skills, soft skills, software tools, and videos on the application business.
- Invest in tools that could help to store and retrieve information on demand. This helps in knowledge management and effective decision making at project or organisation level.
- Ensure newly joined resources in a project also undergo

knowledge transitions. Apart from this, forums—physical or online—can be put in place where business, soft skills, technical issues and solutions are discussed, and some fun activities take place. All these help in making your team competitive and productive as continuous learning culture gets promoted this way.

- Manage capability in your project at all times. Ensure everyone attends training to upskill themselves and remain relevant to business. Use ready templates for organising training plans. Assessment of resources and feedback system for training to be in place. Ready questionnaire, on-the-job training, and reverse KT can be utilised as an evaluation tool for measuring resource's skill proficiency.
- Verification, Pareto analysis, Brainstorming, and other techniques to be utilised on periodic basis to uncover knowledge management issues in a project. Appropriate corrective action plan to be put in place for improving further.
- Ensure lessons learnt and best practices are always documented by the team when working on any projects. These are to be maintained in the organisation tools and utilised by the resources to learn from the past mistakes and do better future planning.

IF YOU ARE NOT
TAKING CARE OF
YOUR CUSTOMER, YOUR
COMPETITOR WILL.
—BOB HOOEY

CHAPTER

09 SURPASSING YOUR COMPETITORS

TODAY THERE are many firms that serve the client by developing systems with the functionality requested by them. However, to survive for a long term you need strategies to stay ahead of your competitors and deliver quality solutions.

This chapter explores the risks like lack of innovation in solutions, lack of customer orientation, not able to retain existing customers through value addition in services, not evaluating critical decisions based on evidence, insufficient automations and reusability initiatives, not giving better postdelivery services, inability to achieve the efficiency in delivery like competitors, and ignoring the non-functional attributes while serving the clients that could lead to issues later.

Risk #94–Lack of innovation in solution

Innovation distinguishes between a leader and a follower.

–Steve Jobs

In any industry, while delivering solutions, innovation is extremely vital to survive long term in business.

Innovation is not just tied to out-of-the-box features, new ideas or concepts but it could easily be done in regular things like improving service delivery packaging, reduction in shipping days of finished products to customers, introducing better pricing, purchasing decision to go for some new hi-tech tools that can drastically reduce effort in solutions, enhancing security and safety features, having better user interface, allowing better integration with different devices and application systems, or eliminating waste in process and automation.

A project which does not practise innovation as a culture is not able to add value to the client or the organisation; it only does repetitive things—consuming same amount of effort or time and ends with wastage in the process. The products developed get vanished in short time and customers switch to the innovative products.

> ***Example:*** **A leading American multinational technology company's smart phones, laptops, or other electronic gadgets have become symbols of innovation. People discard other enterprise products and switch whenever any new product is launched by them.**

Therefore, innovation is a must for permanence in the rapidly changing world. The vendors and their staff members need to adopt this as a culture and implement it in their solutions. *In fact, it is described rightly by Zahra and Covin, 1994, as the lifeblood of the organisation and the only key to survival.*

Prevention strategy

- Discuss with the customers and understand their expectation about desired solutions. Always look for what better technology or process can be adopted in the product development process or in supply chain that can add value to the customers. Understand their pain areas which can also provide you valuable inputs. Also, have a look into the competitors' product and check whether you can do anything better than them.

- In your delivery of services, seek improvement in turnaround time, system availability, warranty, and price. This greatly helps in exceeding client expectations.
- Ask for client approval before proceeding with any innovative idea as your customer may not want to pay extra for some benefits though they are good, due to cost or other factors.
- Discuss innovation strategy in regular review calls with the client and management.
- Have meetings with your project team on regular basis. Seek inputs for improvement in processes and delivery. Abolish process layers which are waste.
- Organisation to enforce innovation in solution through audit checklist or CSAT form.
- Having an idea junction or forum—where resources can contribute their inputs for improvement on a regular basis is extremely helpful.

Risk #95–Not aiming for more business from existing client or lack of customer orientation

Get closer than ever to your customers. So close that you tell them what they need well before they realise it themselves.

–Steve Jobs

The vendor management and team are supposed to work closely with the client and attend to all their work needs on priority. They should have great communication skills, negotiation skills, and technical skills which will ensure customer satisfaction.

No matter how well your team works or how much

knowledge they have, a client will not respect and value it unless you respect them and work according to their expectations and plan.

Great customer orientations are a must for your team. Remember, clients have focus on how you value them and whether you understand their long-term business needs. So, always be accommodative of their needs, prioritise things, and deliver value to your customers.

Prevention strategy

- Maintain portfolio details of your clients with details like service line, location, applications, customer base, their future plans etc. which could be handy in strategic meetings with your leaders.
- Align strategy of your organisation with needs of your customers. This could help you serve them better. Bring improvements in existing operational, infrastructural, marketing, and security measures to win new projects and convince customers about your delivery capabilities and capacities.
- Keep special focus on relationship management with the clients. Every company has few executives who have great influence and are responsible for award of contract to the vendors. Your vendor CEO and leaders need to maintain good and healthy relationship with them.
- Your project team can support your organisation in this by paying special attention to current and future delivery needs of the client, so as to assist them to recover from their pain points and gain new work in the process. However, your organisation needs to carefully assess capabilities and capacities before signing such contracts.
- You can provide value to your client and develop rapport with them by reducing cost at times for your services in

case some business risk is faced by them or give coupons, promotional benefits, loyalty benefits, writing special notes of appreciation, and acknowledgment which can help to nurture the relationship and make it stronger.

> ***Examples:***
>
> *a)* **If you are currently a delivery partner of the client for 'application development' only, look for bidding 'support' projects as well.**
>
> *b)* **You can even suggest solutions in other areas of business like marketing, sales, or finance, which your client might be interested in.**

- New service lines can be introduced by the vendors so as to provide multiple offerings to the clients, thereby eliminating their pain of going to the other vendors.
- Lastly, be with your customer always in their critical times.

Risk #96–Insufficient automation and reusability initiatives

If you aren't using automation you are working too hard.

–Anonymous

Automation is not something new. Many government exams that were once taken on paper and then submitted for manual checking by the examiner have now been made online with evaluation happening as soon as you complete the online test. Thus, developing some software for manual processing work is automation.

Automation is an important aspect that needs to be considered in any project in the modern world. Clients nowadays are very demanding on automations and they want all their vendors to show value additions on yearly basis on these activities. Automation is the future and will help in the long run in running the business of the client at reduced costs, thereby benefitting them in a huge way.

Thus, automation planning is nothing but identifying opportunities for improvements in existing processes or system in a project which will further reduce effort and time for the users. Automations are also considered to provide better convenience to the users or as part of strategic initiative by an organisation.

Examples of automation:

a) **Software system for standards checking, syntax validations, macros for code replacement in program that could make things easy for the engineers.**

b) **Improvement activity in the website of an insurance company allowing customers to do payment online rather than physically visiting their stores.**

c) **HR of a company making attendance system online.**

All these greatly reduce human interventions, making things easy for the customers or users. It profoundly increases the accuracy and reduces spending.

Reusability is nothing but using existing project assets to achieve efficiency in doing some work. This is a way of making use of tools already created by someone and not wasting effort, time, and money to build them again from scratch. This drastically increases performance of the resources and helps them to achieve desired objective easily.

Reusability reduces effort, time, and complexity to a great extent. It eliminates confusion, gives results that are more accurate, and increases profit margin manifold. It increases performance, efficiency, and produces quality product each time. Therefore, reusability strategy is to be planned from initiation of the project itself.

Examples of reusability:

a) **Using existing program, some business logics, or tools that can be used to complete large work in less time.**

b) **Macros with minimal modifications to perform variety of functions.**

c) **Dashboard templates.**

Automation and reusability are implicit needs that may or may not be stated or written as part of the contract but their importance cannot be ignored. Their absence would be a disadvantage to the client in terms of cost, time, effort, quality, and convenience which can make them switch to the other vendors.

Prevention strategy

- Brainstorm with your team for automations that can be sought. Identify the areas in which automation can be done by your project team. It could be reducing the number of lines that you code, switching from manual to automation testing, automation of some processes, optimising jobs and programs consuming lot of CPU time.
- Ask the client for areas in which they seek automation. Quite often, they will tell you upfront what kind of opportunity they foresee in their business.
- Plan for development of in-house tools that can be used to automate the laborious work manually done by resources.
- All automation initiatives need to be reported to the senior management with the objective—savings in terms of efforts, cost, and time with the proposed solution. Automations which are not worth it are to be discarded.

- A repository in a project is to be maintained that contains reusable components or tools like modularised programs, macros, reusable codes, test scripts, and templates.
- Automation and reusability ought to be adopted as an organisation culture. This can be made as a checkpoint in auditor checklist for assessing project and management focus in the same.

Risk #97–Unable to achieve significant margin improvement on yearly basis

Everything is perfect but there is lot of room for improvement.

–Shunryu Suzuki

Most of the clients in this modern world are not looking at the vendors only to carry out regular project activities as mentioned in the scope. Rather they want them as partners who could help them remain relevant in the market and improve their business efficiency. Customers have started thinking long-term and are focused on optimisation and efficiency in carrying out the project activities to achieve savings in costing, effort, and time in future.

At the end of the year, for renewal of a project contract your company should have an edge over other competitors and should be able to provide better pricing, effort reduction, and service quality.

Your vendor company or the project team should come first in the client's mind in terms of better services you provide—knowledge and expertise that your team exhibits, processes you follow, savings realised, ability to communicate well with customers, and above all faster and quality delivery every time. All these when implemented in a project will stop the client from thinking of other vendors, simply because you understood their needs and pain areas best, and provided them quality solutions whenever they were stuck in the past.

Not being able to practise these will lead them to switch to competitors which will be a serious blow to your organisation and you may not know the real reason for the failure of your project.

Prevention strategy

- Ensure automation and reusability strategy initiative is practised on regular basis and reported to the client periodically in status meetings.
- Have complete knowledge of your client's business and application systems. Utilise KEDB and SOPs for faster solution.
- Use your resources well to complete different parts of the deliverables and work collaboratively and efficiently.
- Employ lean principles to remove waste from your processes.
- Critical resources to be identified in a project. Align organisation goal with career goals of these performers. Resources to be appreciated or rewarded for their performance and compensation to be adjusted with the market. Thus, you will be able to retain your good employees and at the same time provide value to the client in terms of faster and defect-free delivery. Also, spending on these resources will certainly be far less than the revenue you will gain from the client over a period of time due to increased capability, leading to high efficiency in operations.
- Promote training and certification in the organisation as a culture, cross-train your resources, ask your employees to come up with ideas and improvements, thereby evaluating and implementing good ideas in the project.
- Innovation, automation, and reusability to be established as a culture.

Risk #98–Unable to achieve the efficiency in operations like competitors

If it cannot be measured, it cannot be managed.

–Peter Drucker

At an organisation level, to stay in business your workforce should work efficiently every minute they are getting billed to achieve better profit margin and develop deliverables with approximately zero post-delivery defects. This is only possible when your team works diligently, and collaborates effectively to perform as a team.

At the project level, to ensure efficiency in operation, we should know what metrics need to be tracked for improvements in process and deliveries. (Refer Appendix-I for some of the common metrics used in project management).

Tracking metrics benefits is directly linked to the key performance indicators (KPIs) which are often tracked by the client and vendor management to assess the project operation and some of them are often a part of the service level agreements.

Metrics that are measured in a project can be broadly categorised into the following:–

- ✓ **Product level**—these metrics directly focus on the product or systems and directly affect customers. Example—defect removal efficiency, defect leakage, delay in milestones, etc.
- ✓ **Process level**—these metrics are used to measure the efficiency and effectiveness of various quality management processes adopted in a project by vendors for developing products or servicing clients. Example—schedule variance (SS), pending request %, review efficiency, KEDB utilisation ratio.
- ✓ **Organisation level**—these may not directly impact the project delivery but are important for the organisation as a whole. Example—gross margin %, return on investments

(ROI), cost, productivity, resource attrition, customer satisfaction, etc.

The three levels discussed above can be utilised to determine nearly all significant metrics that need to be tracked for a project, keeping in mind the project's objective.

These metrics need to have goals defined properly so that the efficiency and effectiveness of processes and delivery quality can be measured. Many professionals simply do not know what their project goals are, or they set incorrect goals which do not lead to any improvements in their service quality.

Metrics goals are to be set considering the current performance of the project team and the competitor performance. These are used to measure the project's success quantitatively.

***Example:* If leading company A needs to be more effective and efficient than its competitors B and C, it should aim for software quality metrics or goals better than them. These could be in terms of product quality, on time delivery, management effectiveness, costing, rates, and customer satisfaction.**

If the vendor project team is delivering below par services, the client may lose interest, stop work, and award that project to the competitors.

Prevention strategy

- Organisation to compute and publish *capability baseline* periodically after analysing trends in the industry and past achievements of the project teams.
- Define the important metrics that you will be tracking in your project after discussion with all the stakeholders.

- Set goals for the metrics defined by utilising the capability baseline mentioned above. Ensure metric goals are higher than what team already meets but not below the market trends.

> ***Examples:***
>
> **a) If competitors 'defect leakage' is 8% your team goal can be 5% (closer to zero indicates better metric);**
>
> **b) If 'defect acceptance ratio' is 95% your team goal can be to meet goal of 97% (closer to 100 indicates better metric).**
>
> **Note: Always aim high!**

- Measure your team performance against these goals. If the team is not able to meet the set goals, then you need to analyse the root cause of the issues and have corrective action in place.
- The significant metrics are to be reported to all the stakeholders—quality assurance team, client, and vendor team for performance achieved with action plan for improvements in future. Any suggestion by them to be incorporated.
- Monitor your performance against these goals periodically until you reach the set goals and when you reach there raise the bar by setting new goals again. Revise actions if need arises in the process. This ensures continual improvements in the projects.

Risk #99–Not able to deliver systems with better attributes

Between two products equal in price, function and quality, the better looking will outsell the other.

–Raymond Loewy

Functional requirements describe what the system should do. Non-functional requirements describe how the system works, often referred to as system qualities.

Today there are many competitors who can build the system with specific behaviours requested by the client, but to maintain edge over them you need to provide better attributes at relatively the same cost or little extra cost.

Examples of attributes:

Operation factors—correctness, reliability, efficiency, integrity, usability.

Revision factors—maintainability, flexibility, and testability.

Transition factors—portability, reusability, and interoperability.

Above classification of requirements is often referred as McCall's factor model.

Non-functional requirements (NFRs) are the enhancers or value-add attributes that the customer expects implicitly or explicitly. These can be a part of the scope but since customers may lack awareness about them, they are often not specified. They are the differentiators in the real world providing you opportunity to exceed client expectation and helping your company to stay in business for long.

Prevention strategy

- If NFRs are not mentioned explicitly as part of the scope document suggest the client for the same and incorporate them as a part of the scope document.
- Utilise new age technologies and tools in products for better look and feel of screens, increased performance, reduced coding for easy maintenance, and easy interface that can be provided to the client application.
- Carefully note all the NFRs as requested by the client,

incorporate these in the design, and implement them to support these functionalities in the software.

- Test your product carefully for all aspects of NFRs and ensure test cases for these are prepared and executed by team. Have independent quality assurance testers to verify any lapses in the process.
- Auditors need to ensure NFRs as mentioned in specification document have been implemented by the project team.
- Note the complaints and suggestions from the customers during warranty. Ensure complaints relevant to NFRs are resolved at the earliest.

Risk #100–Not carefully evaluating the critical decisions and alternatives

Most discussions of decision making assume that only senior executives make decisions or that only senior executives' decisions matter. This is a dangerous mistake.

–Peter Drucker

Critical decisions in a project should not be made only by the senior executives in silos based on own assumptions or what one feels about a given problem but rather it should be with the consensus of the team.

Often, executives are faced with critical decisions such as:-

- ✓ Should the team hire experienced resource from another company or retain existing resources?
- ✓ Should the team go for tool A that gives better performance, better efficiency, medium usability, and high cost or tool B that is freeware, has better usability but not better performance and efficiency than tool A?
- ✓ Should the senior management plan for bidding project X or go for project Y?

There can be many other problems or opportunities like these.

The solution to these questions is not as easy as it may appear. Rather careful evaluation of alternatives is needed. This can be done by gathering data first and weighing relevant parameters with the help of a group. The alternative which is best on above parameters, has minimal risk associated on implementation, and gives maximum advantage is to be selected. *This helps in evidence-based decision making.*

Some of the widely used techniques for evaluating critical decisions like above are weighted tables, pareto analysis, cost-benefit analysis, ranking, brainstorming, decision trees, and six thinking hats.

Not analysing critical decisions using the recommended techniques can lead to wrong alternative selection and cause issues later on in the project or organisation, thereby failing you in meeting project objective.

Prevention strategy

- Organisation QMS needs to have ready templates for various techniques as discussed above, else these need to be created by the decision makers.
- Management or team needs to list the problem definition clearly.
- Once problem definition is drafted, gather data from resources or systems about the problem in question.
- Identify by utilising techniques like brainstorming, focus group, interviewing, etc.—the alternatives that could be the solution.
- Evaluate the different alternatives for the best solution by brainstorming with the team. For this you need to list down the parameters for evaluating them which could be better performance, efficiency, maintainability, cost, security,

productivity, time, effort, etc.

- Weigh them and form a consensus to select the one which has minimum risk and maximum weightage.
- Take formal approval of your senior management or client to proceed with selected alternative and implement it in your project.

Risk #101–Not giving better after-sales service

In the sales profession, the real work begins after the sale is made.

–Brain Tracy

When purchasing your water purifiers, you expect services like installation, periodic checking of water quality,timely candle cleaning and replacement, and its repair from the company that manufactured it. Likewise, the clients seek assistance from the vendors who can solve their problems when any issue arises later.

Though steps are taken by the stakeholders to do thorough testing before acceptance, software issues may not be known; they become evident with time. The client would therefore want someone as a partner who can help their business users when any issue comes up in the live environment.

Software can have lots of technicalities and users may not know how to use it. They would want someone who can help their team or business users to understand their application system and resolve their queries.

At the same time, software like any other product comes with an expiry date. Customers can experience performance issues while using it. Some regulatory requirements could change and adjustments for the same may be required by the customers in the application system to remain relevant in the business.

There could be strategic reasons like to capture the market by going first. So, clients could have time constraints and they would like to roll-out their first version of the product live as soon as possible with features that provide the most business value to them.

Therefore, better after-sales services like warranty, user training and support, and upgrade service are the prime criteria when customers are selecting prospective vendors.

Prevention strategy

- Set the warranty period in the contract before beginning the project. This should vary based on complexity and size of the product. For example—this could vary from one month to six months for medium to large system. Warranty period can be in years too, for large projects.
- Maintain all defects received in the warranty period and ensure that not many defects by customers are realised in this phase. All such defects to be fixed immediately with minimum impact on users.
- Analyse the root cause of such issues and correct any potential fault in the system that could cause further problems for users.
- Vendor management needs to pay attention to the number of warranty issues and relevant metrics to access the quality of delivery by the team. Appropriate corrective action plan to be in place to improve existing processes and relationship with the client.
- Never forget to update the service manual and helping documentation for changes in warranty.
- Ensure you provide training and support for the usage of software product if requested. You can arrange a meeting and give them physical demo, or through online mediums like WebEx, Zoom, or upload the video of its usage on

internet—YouTube, LinkedIn, Facebook, etc.—where users are in large number and can spread across a vast area.

- Upgrade services to be provided to existing clients at reduced price.

APPENDIX-I

Few common metrics used in project management:

Gross margin %—gives the profit percentage that can be realised as part of a given project or contract. These metrics are to be set in the planning stages and should be monitored during various phases of the project. For eg 20% of project revenue to be made as part of profit for upcoming project.

Gross Margin % = ((total project revenue – total cost)/total project revenue) *100

Defect Removal Efficiency—also, known as DRE, gives measure of ability of development team to close defects raised during testing cycle with QA team.

For example if defects raised by QA team are 100 and 65 defects are closed by development team, then DRE= 65/100 = 65%.

Pending request %—percentage of tickets not yet closed by team out of total received in a given period.

Pending request % = (no of pending tickets completed in period/total tickets received in that period) *100

Defect leakage percentage—indicates defects percentage leaked to customer out of total internal defects.

Leakage percentage = (customer defect/(internal+customer defect)) *100

Schedule slippage—indicates number of days by which delivery is late from planned date of delivery.

SS = (actual delivery date – planned delivery date) converted into days

Effort variance %—gives the variation of actual effort vs the estimated effort. It is actually used to measure the efficiency of team in carrying out the work allocated as per the planned effort.

Effort variance = (actual effort – estimated effort /estimated effort) *100

GLOSSARY

A

Acceptance criteria

Mostly given by the client, defines list of conditions to be met before declaring work is complete. Often it is given for validating user stories or as part of testing.

B

Background verification (BGV)

The process of verifying education, family, career, and social background of the prospects, prior to hiring them in projects or organisation. This helps in preventing criminal activities and filtering doubtful candidates.

Baseline

Accepted and approved specification or product that serves as the basis for further development. It can be changed only through formal change control procedures. Example—project plan created by team needs to be formally approved by stakeholders before using it as a base for carrying out development activities.

Boundary value analysis (BVA)

The process of testing between extreme ends of range of input values. Minimum, maximum, just inside, just outside, and a nominal value are used to test the software product.

Business as usual (BAU)

Often used in business it implies to continue normal operations as earlier or let things continue in normal or usual way.

Business case

A justification detailing the benefits in terms of return on investment (ROI), saving in effort, time, convenience, user experience, market value, and competitive advantage elaborating why certain project is worth an investment. All the benefit parameters mentioned above should be quantified in a business case so that outcome can be easily measured and compared.

Business users

End-users who will finally use the application developed for performing the business functions.

C

Capability

Intangible assets of an organisation. These are quite different from basic and tangible resources required for production like infrastructure, people, application or financial capital. In fact, capability is the skill that is based on knowledge, experience, and information which controls resources of production as mentioned above. A company with more experienced and knowledgeable people, better processes documentation and control in place, and a good management team can take better informed decisions and deliver quality products/services.

Capability baseline

A snapshot of the organisation process capability achieved at some point of time. It gives the control limit for each process that can be implemented by project. It helps in setting goal for the project metrics which determine success of the organisation operation. Refer risk #98 for more details.

Capability maturity model integration (CMMI)
It is a well-accepted model in software industry. It gives a ready set of processes which an organisation can put in place for effectiveness in operations.

Capacity
Capacity planning is done to determine the amount of work that can be delivered in specified time with available human resources, capital, facilities, and equipment of a company.

Change management process
After the scope is defined and approved new changes to the existing product scope are to be accommodated by the change management process for acceptance. The change management process usually has appropriate authority or members called change advisory board (CAB) to approve the changes only after properly evaluating them.

Change request (CR)
A document with any new changes asked by the client after scope is baselined; such changes to be controlled and considered through change management process.

Clarification logs
Refer risk #13

Client
It refers to anyone who buys professional services and advice from a person or business.

Colocation
Seating arrangement for the project team members in the same floor or building, so that they can collaborate better and work more efficiently.

COBIT 5
It is a framework that is used for the management and governance of information technology.

Configuration management

Organising, controlling, and maintaining the service assets like hardware, software, and artifacts used during the project life cycle so as to establish consistency in process and improving performance. This helps to provide service with minimal mistakes and with productivity. Example—tracking and controlling the changes in the software system, design, test cases, etc. It also helps in easy restoration of system to its earlier running state.

Crashing

The addition of resources to a project to meet project schedule. However, it increases the project cost.

Critical path method (CPM) or Critical path analysis

A widely used technique in project management. Helps to figure out the shortest time in which a project can be completed. The activities which are in critical path require more focus from organisation while those not in the path can be completed in parallel with some other activities. It is of strategic importance to organisation as it leads to effective utilisation of resources, saves on project costing, opportunity cost, revenue maximisation, etc.

Cross-training

A project needs resources with different skill sets. Team members with expertise in one skill set or business functions can train others to prepare them for future engagements and sharing workload.

Cross-skilling

Making resources multi-skilled so that employees can take position other than one for which they are hired. It gives strategic advantage to organisation to meet on-demand needs of customers and remaining relevant to business.

Customer

Organisation or individual who purchases goods or services. In IT organisations, client and customer are often used interchangeably.

D

Deliverable

Final output like design, test case, end product, etc. that goes to customers. It can be tangible or intangible asset.

Disruptions

Any event that brings extensive change in an industry, business strategy, or in other aspects especially involving the introduction of a new technology, product or service; this often leads to creation of new markets.

E

Equivalence class partitioning (ECP)

This technique can be used for black or white box testing. Set of valid input values are divided into partitions which have equal behaviour when processing is done on them. The valid partitions (range of given input values) and the invalid partitions (not allowed input values usually beyond range) are tested for ensuring product developed is as per expectation.

Estimation

This is used to give ball park figure of effort required to complete a given project or task. This is an important part of planning in project management as it gives rough idea of when the project will be completed, its cost and resource needs. For meaning and techniques like expert judgement, analogous estimates, three-point estimates or PERT estimates, and parametric estimates, refer risk #81.

F

Fast tracking

This technique in project management involves the execution of activities in parallel to complete project on time. However, the risk factor gets increased.

Full-time employees (FTEs)

Employees who are usually on client's payroll but are allocated to work on some project with vendor team as part of contract. They usually work on deliverables, review, or coordinate with vendor project teams, and share responsibilities.

G

Gold plating

Refer risk #17.

I

Interested parties

Refer risk #73.

Interoperability

The ability of software system to interact and work in coordination with other operating system, software, and tools.

ISO (International organisation for standardisation)

Worldwide standard-setting body with representatives from various national standard organisations. It sets standards in many businesses and technologies, including computing and communications.

ISO 9000

Presents the set of standards on quality management and quality assurance that can be adopted by any organisation to maintain an efficient quality system. It includes the seven quality management principles upon which the family of standards is based.

ISO 9001

Family of quality management standards within ISO 9000. One of the most coveted certifications for organisations around the world.

ISO 27001

Represents standard for information security management system.

K

Key performance indicator (KPI)

Success of organisation, project, or employee can be measured by setting parameters which are quantifiable. These can then be used to evaluate whether management has met their objectives.

Kick-off meeting

A meeting organised for the first time between the client and project team for planning project activities, understanding responsibilities, and establishing commitments from all the stakeholders.

Known error data base (KEDB)

Refer risk #67

M

Manager

A person who is accountable for project success. He is the overall in-charge of the planning and execution of a particular project. A leader in organisation to whom resources assigned to the project, called as project team, directly report day-to-day operations.

Master service agreement (MSA)

A legal contract that governs relationship between the service provider and client. (Refer beginning of chapter 2 for more details).

Minimal viable product (MVP)

Most pared down version of a product that can still be deployed and has sufficient features to satisfy customers. Complete versions can be developed in stages after feedback by customer or business users.

O

Objectives

Objectives are the business benefits that organisation expects to achieve on investing time and effort to complete a project.

These are different from project output—deliverables and work products. Needs to be decided by vendor management during project planning. These can include parameters like budget, quality, time to completion, and return on investment (ROI).

Operational level agreements (OLA)

These are internal agreements between the departments, application teams, and other stakeholders for providing services associated for particular project. Usually these are set to meet service level agreement (SLA) set by the client.

Opportunity cost

It is the cost of not investing in the next better opportunity available at hand or another project available for investment, often given up due to lack of time and resources to execute it, because of first project selection.

Outcome

Results desired from a project. This includes not just the tangible results like software product or intermediate deliverables produced during the project but also intangible things like business value and benefits provided to client.

Outsourcing

It is a practice in which one company contracts with another company for undertaking its services or manufacturing some product which could have been developed in-house. This strategy is mainly employed to reduce cost but can be for various other strategic reasons.

P

Pareto analysis

A statistical technique based on pareto principle or 80/20 rule which states 80% of the effects come from 20% of the causes. Often used as a part of decision making to come up with top action points for maximum impact.

Phase-gate process or stage-gate process

Refer risk #24

Portfolio

These are set of projects or program which are strategically organised to analyse the potential returns of undertaking a project. They share common business objectives and goals. It helps to manage projects whose outcomes are interdependent on one another.

Program

A group of related projects managed in a coordinated manner to obtain benefits which cannot be obtained from managing them individually.

Project

A temporary endeavour which is unique and has definite outcome.

Project team

Resources assigned to the project like developers, testers, or functional consultants who carry out the project activities as part of contract. They directly report to the project manager.

Proof of concept (POC)

An experiment or pilot project run to determine feasibility of given idea, business case, or business proposal.

Q

Quality assurance (QA)

A way of ensuring that right processes are in place to deliver solution to client with minimal defect and bring value to the organisation. Firms ensure various verification and validation activities are in place to meet this purpose. Example—testing, auditing, facilitations, reviews, etc.

It's also a generic term that can be used to refer to departments and professionals accountable to ensure quality.

Quality control (QC)

Narrower term than Quality Assurance as it's mostly product-centered. All testing activities mentioned as a part of test plan like Unit, SIT, etc. are quality control activities.

Quality management system (QMS)

A documented set of processes, standards, guidelines, and procedures to be followed in organisation while planning and execution of projects.

R

RACI Model, RACI Matrix, or Responsibility accountable matrix (RAM)

A model that is widely used during delegation of tasks to avoid confusion. Resources assigned can take following roles—responsible, accountable, consulted and informed. It also helps in better task reporting and avoids role confusion amongst resources.

Reliability

It is the ability of software system to operate without faults or errors for a given period of time, in a given environment.

Reusability

Any project or organisation asset that can be reused to increase efficiency of resources or system. This includes existing program, codes, designs, test scripts, macro, process documents, checklist, and standards.

Reverse engineering

It is a process in which existing system is analysed by understanding its behaviours, attributes and architecture, and documenting the principles of its working. Mostly done in cases where system source code or documentation is no more available.

Request for information (RFI)
Refer risk #33

Request for proposal (RFP)
Refer risk #33

RFQ (Request for quote) or (Invitation for bid)
Refer Risk #33

Risk and Opportunity
There are various factors—internal or external to project, that can impact it in positive or negative ways. Those that can bring negative outcome are risks and those that bring positive outcome on objectives are opportunities. Both of these can be captured as risk in project risk tracker.

Rollback
The process of restoring a database or program to a previously defined state typically to recover from an error.

Root cause analysis (RCA)
A systematic process used in identifying the primary reason of the faults in the system or any problems is called RCA. Usually involves brainstorming and analysing the related incidents, defects, or issues in the project. This is then used to plan corrective action and permanently fix the issue.

S

Scope
Refer beginning of chapter 2.

Scope creep
Refer risk #16.

Senior management
These are bosses in the company with role above the project manager. They are responsible for supporting project managers within their portfolio with execution of project and represent organisation interest.

Service asset
These include hardware, software tools and applications, buildings, people, artifacts, formal documentation, etc. that help to deliver services to the customers or business.

Service provider
Any organisation that provides consulting, legal, processing, or storage service to customers.

Service level agreement (SLA)
Refer risk #64

Six Sigma
Set of techniques and tools for process improvement introduced by engineer Bill Smith while working at Motorola in 1980. Helps to identify causes of defects and minimises variability in business processes and manufacturing.

Statement of work (SOW)
Refer risk #10.

Sponsor
A person or organisation that is funding the project.

SPOC
Single point of contact.

Stakeholders
Anyone who has direct or indirect interest in project outcome. Example—sponsors, client manager, vendor management, project team, HR, admin, etc.

Standards operating procedures (SOP)
Refer risk #67.

Subject matter expert (SME)
Anyone having expertise in the technical, domain, product, or application system.

Supplier
Refer risk #33.

T

Third parties
Refer risk #73.

V

Vendor
Any company or person that is contracted by client/customer to provide some service to them.

W

Work break-down structure (WBS)
Breaking down of a large work request into smaller tasks or activities. This is often accompanied by ordering them or grouping them to form sections that can be easily managed.

Work product
Smallest level of output tracked for a project. A deliverable like final requirement or design can be made of several work products. These can be tangible or intangible assets.

SOURCES OF INFORMATION

Best practices shared in this book are referenced from the CMMI, ISO, PMP, ITIL, COBIT, etc. Author has taken great pains in ensuring 100% original content and written the book based on his own knowledge and the experience gained over the years in the professional world. However, any resemblance in lines or content could be coincidental.

The author of the book is thankful to all the writers whose published articles have been used in the book. Their writing makes a difference in peoples' lives and I believe their message will spread even more. This will help in creating more entrepreneurs and bringing success in the life of professionals and students.

All the brand names of products, softwares, and companies used in this book are trademarks and IP of the respective owners. These names are used as reference only.

The author or publisher do not endorse any specific products, softwares and services in any manner whatsoever.

REFERENCES

1. https://faethcoaching.com/it-project-failure-rates-facts-and-reasons/
   Some Project Management Facts of Real World
   (Introduction)
2. https://en.wikipedia.org/wiki/Volatility,_uncertainty,_complexity_and_ambiguity
   (Introduction)
3. https://projectmanagementinsight.com/business-case-or-requirements/
   Karen Munro, blogger, Project Management Insight
   (Risk #11)
4. https://www.pmi.org/learning/library/requirements-management-planning-for-success-9669
   Tim Coventry, CEO for Business Analysts Pty Ltd (BAPL)
   (Risk #13)
5. https://pmstudycircle.com/2012/09/scope-creep-and-gold-plating-in-project-management/
   Fahad Usmani, Author, PMP, PMI-RMP
   (Risk #16 and Risk #17)
6. https://resources.workfront.com/project-management-blog/how-to-write-a-business-case-4-steps-to-a-perfect-business-case-template
   Martin Webster, IT professional
   (Risk #18)

7. https://www.entrepreneur.com/article/252061
The 10 Things You Need to Know When Responding to RFPs
George Deeb, Managing Partner at Red Rocket Ventures
(Risk #20)

8. http://blogs.sas.com/content/sascom/2015/05/26/how-to-prevent-a-failed-proof-of-concept/
Muhammad Asif Abbasi, Principal Business Solutions Manager
(Risk #21)

9. https://www.invensis.net/blog/it/advantages-and-disadvantages-of-dotnet-and-java/
Arvind Rongala, Manager, Business Development, and Marketing, for Invensis Technologies
(Risk #34)

10. https://www.upguard.com/blog/5-configuration-management-boss
Upguard.com
(Risk #40)

11. https://melsatar.blog/2012/03/21/choosing-the-right-software-development-life-cycle-model/
Mohamed Sami, certified Enterprise Architect
(Risk #42)

12. https://www.contractstandards.com/public/clauses/force-majeure
(Risk #71)

13. https://www2.deloitte.com/global/en/pages/governance-risk-and-compliance/articles/third-party-risk.html
Kristian Park, Deloitte LLP in the United Kingdom
(Risk #73)

14. http://technacon.com/iso9001/interested-parties.htm
Sherri Gallagher, Quality and Industrial Engineering

Consultant at Technacon Company Inc

(Risk #73)

15. http://www.eqavet.eu/qc/gns/glossary/s/stakeholders.aspx

(Risk #73)

16. https://www.metricstream.com/insights/best-practices-third-party-mgmt-program.htm

(Risk #76)

17. http://usabilitygeek.com/the-difference-between-usability-and-user-experience/
Justin Mifsud, Founder of UsabilityGeek, visiting lecturer with the University of Hertfordshire

(Risk #79)

18. http://softwaretestingfundamentals.com/test-case/

(Risk #85)

19. http://qatestlab.com/resources/knowledge-center/why-are-test-data-important-for-quality-software-testing/

(Risk #87)

ABOUT THE AUTHOR

MANOJ YADAV holds MLE^{SM} title and is a president's select member of 'Leaders Excellence', a business leader's community at Harvard Square, Massachusetts, USA. He has numerous global professional certifications to his credit, namely ITIL Foundation certified from AXELOS (UK), PMP certified from PMI (USA), ISO 9001:2015, certification from DNV GL (Norway) and is a trained CMMI professional.

He is an IT veteran with 14+ years' rich diverse work experience in Business Excellence, Project Management, Business Analyst, and Technology services of organisation. He has served Fortune 500 clients like American Express, Humana Inc, and AmerisourceBergen in his roles with MNCs—IBM, AtoS Syntel, Patni Computer Systems, and Lionbridge.

He has audited around 150+ projects, thereby interviewing 300+ managers and leaders, enabled them to improve operations so as to exceed customer satisfaction and improved profit margin of the organisation. His book *101 Secrets Of Project Risk Management* is a pioneer work on IT Risk Management, where for the first time he is detailing in-depth around 98% risks affecting projects and strategies to mitigate them. It is an innovative book on project, quality, and risk management which is useful for various industries.

An alumnus of one of the top engineering institute VJTI, Mumbai University, he graduated in BE Computer Engineering. He also holds certification in Finance and Marketing from Emory University (USA) and University of Illinois at Urbana-Champaign (USA) respectively. Apart from these, he has certifications in life and general insurance from reputed Insurance Institute of India (III) and multiple finance certifications from premier National Institute of Security Markets (NISM), India.

He is amongst the top writers of knowledge sharing social media website, Quora, and has reach of 1,00,000+ readers across the globe. He resolves queries and doubts of professionals and students in leadership and management space. He is a people's person who loves to inspire and has written more than 100 motivational quotes on success. He has a network of 13,500+ people following him on LinkedIn.

A multi-talented personality, he is good in various activities like singing, dialogue delivery, and sports like carrom, table tennis, chess, etc.